MW01013184

The Right Side of the Table

Where Do You Sit in the Minds of the Affluent?

The Right Side of the Table

Where Do You Sit in the Minds of the Affluent?

By Scott Fithian and Todd Fithian

Written with Jennifer Summer Tolman

The Financial Planning Association (FPA) is the membership association for the financial planning community. FPA is committed to providing information and resources to help financial planners and those who champion the financial planning process succeed. FPA believes that everyone needs objective advice to make smart financial decisions.

FPA Press is the publishing arm of FPA, providing current content and advanced thinking on technical and practice management topics.

Financial Planning Association
4100 Mississippi Ave., Suite 400
Denver, Colorado 80246-3053

Phone: 800.322.4237
Fax: 303.759.0749
E-mail: fpapress@fpanet.org

www.fpanet.org

ISBN: 0-9753448-9-7
ISBN-13: 978-0-9753448-9-7

Manufactured in the United States of America

This book is dedicated to Arlene, Matthew, and Michael Fithian, Scott's wife and sons, and to Debbie, Andrew, Ryan, and Kelly Fithian, Todd's wife and children, for their unwavering support of the long hours and near obsession with which we have pursued our vision for change in the financial services industry.

It is also dedicated to the members of the Legacy Wealth Coach Network: hundreds of incredible men and women who have used our methodology with wealth holders and, seeing the transformation that occurs, have applied their behaviors and their influence to help spread the word about a better way to plan.

About the Authors

Scott C. Fithian was widely recognized as a pioneer in the financial services industry. As a young adviser, he always challenged the conventional philosophy and methodology that had been the foundation for the industry long before his own Dad had started his career in the business. He always felt there was a better way to achieve the desired results for his clients while greatly increasing their satisfaction in the relationship.

Scott spent his career developing proprietary tools, systems and strategies that were designed to put the client's vision, mission and values at the center of the planning process. His visionary approach made him a sought after public speaker throughout the U.S. and Canada, and a popular contact for leading edge research, insights, and commentary.

In 1996, Scott launched the Legacy Companies so he could share his unique perspective with other financial advisers in order to create positive industry change. Over the next ten years, Scott would train thousands of advisers in his values-based client centered approach to planning.

In 2000, Scott published his acclaimed book *Values-Based Estate Planning*. The book became a must-read for the adviser who was looking to follow in Scott's footsteps and build deeper, more meaningful relationships with their clients. In 2004, Scott became an executive producer on the film, "The Ultimate Gift"—a film that celebrates the special relationship between an adviser and his client.

Scott's brilliant career was shortened in September 2006 after a courageous 18-month battle with cancer. Throughout his illness, he remained passionate about his beliefs and desires to make a lasting difference on the financial services industry. Scott worked on *The Right Side of the Table* until a month before he passed, and it represents his most current and final perspective on the topic.

Today, Scott's legacy lives on through the countless advisers he touched over the years and through the business he started with his brother Todd. A true visionary in the industry, Scott's ideas and concepts can be found throughout the financial services community and beyond.

Todd Fithian has literally grown up in the financial services industry. As a member of the third generation of the family in the industry, Todd, along with his late brother Scott, was always driven to approach things a little differently than their predecessors. As Todd often puts it, by starting at a different place, more effective, lasting results will certainly be delivered.

A lifelong entrepreneur, Todd formed his own financial advisory firm in Boston soon after graduating from the University of Massachusetts. Todd then joined forces with his brother Scott in 1996 to form the Legacy Companies, a consulting company for professional advisers to learn and implement the Fithians' proprietary "Discovery Process." As co-developer of the Legacy Wealth Optimization System®, Todd has consulted with advisers, business owners, corporations, and families in the U.S., Canada, and Australia.

Today, Todd is the CEO of the Legacy Companies and a frequent speaker on the subject of client discovery and sustainability. Although not as often as he would like, Todd continues to spend time consulting with business owners and families, leading them through their own Discovery Processes.

Todd and his wife Debbie have two sons and a daughter. When he's away from his work, Todd is often found in a hockey rink, behind the bench, coaching his two sons' teams.

Jennifer Summer Tolman owns a marketing firm in Pacifica, California, called Second Summer Inc. She supports top professional advisers working in the affluent marketplace in the areas of ghost writing, brand development, and referral coaching.

Acknowledgments

There is a very, very long list of important people who have positively impacted our lives, without whom this book would never have been completed. We cannot possibly list them all here, but we hope you know who you are.

To Curt and Jane Fithian—your constant love, guidance, support, wisdom, and patience made us who we are today. We are so proud to call you Mom and Dad.

We must recognize four individuals who have made significant and valuable contributions to our work and ultimately helped shape the thinking shared in this book. A tremendous, heartfelt thank you goes out to Dr. Paul Schervish, Dan Sullivan, Jim Stovall, and Jennifer Summer Tolman.

We have been extremely blessed to have such wonderful clients, friends, clients who have become friends, strategic partners, investors, and family who have made our work so fulfilling and rewarding. Thank you to all of you for making our work not feel like work at all.

We could not have accomplished a thing without our tremendous team of people at the Legacy Companies: Donn Worby, Rob Falvey, Tom Kennedy, Tom Holland, Susan Denisevich, Naomi Grossack, Jen Thiboutot, Holly Dubay, Jessica Reichert, and John McAnespie.

Thank you to Mary Corbin, our talented editor at FPA Press who exercised amazing patience with us as we completed a book that was a lot more difficult to get done than we ever anticipated. We couldn't have done this without you, Mary.

Finally, we are very grateful and appreciative that we had such a tremendous group of advisers who reviewed our manuscript and provided tremendous insights and advice that helped push the book across the finish line. A special thank you to:

Timothy J. Belber, JD
Jeffrey M. Holler, CFP®
Brian McNulty
Richard Phillips, CFP®
James Barnash, CFP®

About FPA

The Financial Planning Association® (FPA®) is the membership organization for the financial planning community. FPA is built around four Core Values—Competence, Integrity, Relationships, and Stewardship. We want as members those who share our Core Values.

FPA's primary aim is to be the community that fosters the value of financial planning and advances the financial planning profession. The FPA strategy to accomplish its objectives involves welcoming all those who advance the financial planning process and promoting the CERTIFIED FINANCIAL PLANNER™ (CFP®) marks as the cornerstone of the financial planning profession. FPA is the heart of financial planning, connecting those who deliver, support, and benefit from it.

FPA was created on the foundation that the CFP marks best represent the promise and the future of the financial planning profession. CFP certification offers the public a consistent and credible symbol of professional competence in financial planning. And FPA benefits the public by helping to ensure that financial planning is delivered through competent and ethical financial planners.

FPA members include individuals and companies who are dedicated to helping people make wise financial decisions to achieve their life goals and dreams. FPA believes that everyone needs objective advice to make smart financial decisions and that when seeking the advice of a financial planner, the planner should be a CFP professional.

FPA is committed to improving and enhancing the professional lives and capabilities of our members. We offer a variety of programs and services to that end.

Table of Contents

Foreword by Dan Sullivan ....xiv–xvi

Introduction 1

Chapter 1: The Wealth Holder's Mind Is a Curious Thing 5

Chapter 2: The Right Side of the Table 11

Chapter 3: The Chairs Are Changing 23

Chapter 4: The Three Adviser Styles 31

Chapter 5: Choosing the Right Chair 43

Chapter 6: Why Planning Fails: The Four Key Obstacles and the Confidence Formula Solution 49

Chapter 7: The Most Trusted Adviser vs. the Specialist/ Expert 65

Chapter 8: The Intentional Team Model: The Core Team, the Virtual Team, and the Role of the Specialist/Expert 77

Chapter 9: Seats and Compensation 89

Chapter 10: What Now? *By Todd Fithian* 99

Epilogue: Reflections from Scott C. Fithian 103

Index: 109

Foreword

I had the privilege to know Scott Fithian during the ten years when he was at his most creative, productive and influential. During the late 1990s, I had the opportunity to see, in depth, the remarkable program of training that he was providing to financial advisers across the U.S. and Canada. During this same period, I knew dozens of financial advisers who were students of Scott's. They all reported how much their perspectives and capabilities were being transformed by their involvement with Scott's concepts, strategies, and processes.

Looking back, it's an easy claim to make that Scott's transformative work fundamentally changed the way that thousands of financial advisers approach their clientele and professional practices. He was a pioneer and creative leader of the concept of "client-centered" financial advisory. I can remember dozens of conversations with Scott where he laid out for me his innovative principles that, in many ways, ran completely counter to the commodity-based training that advisers received in most financial services companies. I remember him telling me, "The whole marketplace is shifting. The clients are taking the control away from the head office bureaucrats. The advisers better make up their mind quickly whose side they are on."

It was very clear to me that Scott had made up his mind. He was always on the clients' side. And he was always on the side of those advisers who committed themselves to their clients.

The title of this book, therefore, perfectly sums up Scott's approach—looking at things entirely through the clientele's eyes. Being on the "right side" of the table, for Scott, meant forgetting about what you wanted to sell. The question was what did the client want to achieve? What dangers did clients have that they wanted to eliminate? What opportunities did they want to capture? What strengths did they want to maximize? Above all, what was the big picture that clients had for themselves, for their families, and for their businesses? Scott's approach looked at clients as whole human beings who had concerns and aspirations that spanned their own lifetimes and beyond.

Along with my work with Scott, I've also had the opportunity to cooperate and create with thousands of advisers—many of whom were trained by Scott. All advisers are different, they each have their own personality and their own chemistry with particular types of clients. But among those who are truly client-centered, there are some crucial characteristics in common. They are great listeners and they succeed by asking great questions. My own sense is that among the ranks of the most successful client-centered advisers are some of the best natural psychologists in the world. They truly have the capability of seeing the client's world through the client's eyes. Scott Fithian had this quality, and so do a great many of the advisers that he trained.

Probably the biggest thing that all client-centered advisers share is a particular quality of client. These clients are very intelligent, successful, multi-dimensional individuals who demand custom-designed service in all areas of their lives. For that reason, only a certain kind of adviser will be acceptable to them.

I know many of these advisers and here's what they tell me their clients want: First of all, an approach that enables them (the clients) to think about all of their problems and issues—not just those related to their finances. Next, they want a greater sense of direction, confidence, and capability in all areas of their lives. Because of this, they want financial strategies to be part of much larger lifetime solutions. When it comes to solutions, they want everything based on their issues and concerns, not on the adviser's need for commissions. It's very important to these clients that the advisers are independent of bureaucratic dependencies. They want someone whose loyalty and commitment is to them, not to a corporation. It reassures them to know that the advisers are personally successful and confident. They place great value on long-term relationships. For this reason, they want financial advisers who can help them construct a lifetime plan and then be there continually to help them implement it.

All of these requirements are, of course, integral to Scott's philosophy and approach. These characteristics describe who his clients were—and how he served them. They also describe the framework that Scott created, so that other advisers could be successful with the very best quality of clientele.

When I first started working with successful financial advisers in 1974, the very first client I worked with had a plaque on his wall with the following message on it: “If you would sell what John Smith buys, you must see through John Smith’s eyes.”

The adviser, who was a legend among life insurance agents, noticed that I was reading it. “You know,” he said, “very few people in our industry ever understand this. They’re always trying to sell something. Me? I’m always buying something. When I meet with clients, I’m always buying their life and their future. Their worries and their aspirations. Once the clients realize that I’ve bought everything that means the most to them, they give me all their business.”

Scott Fithian was another legend who was a buyer rather than a seller. He always saw through John Smith’s eyes. That’s why he always ended up on the right side of the table. I encourage as many financial advisers as possible to join him there.

—Dan Sullivan
Founder of The Strategic Coach
Toronto, July 24, 2007

Introduction: The Right Side of the Table

When each of us decided to become a financial adviser, we took a step in a very specific direction. We chose to advise people on one of the most important aspects of their lives. Some of us got into the business on purpose; some took a first job and stayed for decades. The world has become a very different place than it was back then. Millions of people are becoming surprisingly wealthy, and their opportunities and contemplations are mounting. What will you do to be a student of the business—to rise to the occasion of your consumers' changing needs?

In an industry where intelligence and entrepreneurial ability has allowed thousands of men and women to achieve tremendous financial success, we now face an introspection point. Innovation—both accidental and intentional—has led our businesses in specific directions. Which services have you chosen to offer and why? Today, there is a greater responsibility than ever before to be intentional and to communicate that intent to our clients.

If you focus on one key area, do you tell your clients to seek out their missing services elsewhere, even though the professionals they engage may be your competitors? Or will the family remain exposed in a crucial area because no one brought it to their attention? A lack of action still demonstrates intent; it still carries consequences for the consumer.

So whether you got here by accident or on purpose, through brilliance or sheer tenacity, today, we believe every financial services professional has an obligation to the consumers of our products and services: to honestly and introspectively settle into his or her own right role. Change and innovation is good as long as it matches your skill set. We must evaluate what services we provide, how we are compensated for those services, and how both of these serve the consumer's ideal ultimate ends.

The title of this book introduces a metaphor surrounding the proverbial conference room table. It suggests that as wealth increases in our society, wealth holders are demanding a different model for assembling their team of professional advisers. Team members will take specific seats at the table, next to or across from the wealth holder, based on the role they are best suited to play. As more and more advisers adopt authenticity in their selection, wealth holders will become savvier to those trying to disguise their underlying relationship goals. Advisers must be clear about where they're meant to sit and why.

It's also about helping our clients get to the root of *their* intent. So much of financial services is focused on tax savings and tax elimination. Yet, for people who have exceeded financial independence, that can't possibly be their ultimate goal for their wealth. How could it? Life has so much more to offer.

To help wealth holders find the true intent for their wealth requires deep discovery, skillful discovery. It requires conversations in which there isn't a single product idea, service mix, or technical strategy dangling in the back of the adviser's mind. The quality of the wealth holder's choices increases in direct proportion to the quality of discovery used to facilitate them. It's a philosophy that we have proven time and time again with self-made men and women, widows, and recipients of second-generation wealth. A person is best equipped to make a wise choice if the adviser poses enough of the right questions. Not ideas, questions. Ask, listen, ask deeper, and listen more intently. Let the conversation flow naturally toward the client's own ah-ha. That's how they find their ultimate intent for their wealth. This is a discernment-based style of communication, which is the foundation of our teachings and of this book. We believe that soon there will be a discernment-based adviser at every planning table.

Because there is more money in more peoples' hands than ever before in our society, we also have a greater obligation to effectively steward the impact of the transactions we're stimulating. It's great to get $10 million down to the kids tax-free. Now what's going to happen to them when they receive it? We can turn our backs and move on to the next, or we can change the trajectory of the meaning of wealth in this country. We can coach the parents and mentor the kids or bring in other professionals who do this. Regardless of how it gets done, we owe it to our clients to create opportunities, not messes, for their heirs. In the right side of the table model, successful advisers will embrace an abundance mentality, inviting additional advisers to the table to fill roles the core team isn't suited to play.

This book was written to help advisers in a variety of business life cycles make an intentional choice about the next decades of their careers. Our hope is that you can be still with yourself and use the information here to find your ideal resting point—a perfect match between what you are meant to do in this world and the direct needs of the marketplace. We hope you'll approach this journey in a discovery-based mindset—not looking for confirmation of what you already know or hope to find out, but seeing what presents itself.

As you work through the chapters, you'll encounter specific terminology and net worth brackets. These were developed based on our personal experiences in working with high-wealth families, as well as the experiences of thousands of advisers across the United States and Canada whom we have trained in our philosophy. If you find yourself disagreeing with the terminology or the way we have sectioned off the marketplace, try to set those opinions aside and soak up the message. At its core, this book is a report on the behaviors and experiences that occur when a high-end adviser sits down to help an affluent family plan. It's about how we can improve the family's experiences in planning by changing certain behaviors. We believe everyone can learn something from what we share in these pages.

Two of the terms you'll encounter are central to what we've learned over several decades of doing this work and teaching it to thousands of others. The first is *wealth holder*. We use this in place of client. It refers to people who have exceeded financial independence or who are on their way to doing so. The term was designed to show deep respect and compassion for the challenges and complexities that a person of wealth faces. Where "client" is a sales or business term, wealth holder is about the individual life we're attempting to affect. As the industry evolves, wealth holders are regaining their rightful power. They are becoming savvier about who plays what role at their planning table, and what financial incentives exist behind the scenes. If advisers don't choose their seats with authenticity, the wealth holder will do it for them.

The second crucial term is *most trusted adviser*. It refers to an individual who is selected on purpose by the wealth holder to oversee all of their affairs and all of their advisers. Before you say to yourself, "yes, that's me," we hope you'll read this book. Our definition of most trusted adviser is something our industry is growing toward, not something that completely exists today in all wealth brackets.

As you read the following chapters, review the table diagram and consider where you've been sitting all these years. Consider the services you offer and how you charge for your services. Have these choices influenced the wealth holder's perception of you? Have they influenced the effectiveness of the process? *The Right Side of the Table* model requires full disclosure and increased authenticity regarding compensation and expertise. The opportunities for professional advisers are tremendous. The time has come to make an intentional and wise choice. Which is the right side of the table for you?

1 *The Wealth Holder's Mind Is a Curious Thing*

CHAPTER AT A GLANCE:

There is one primary force driving the shifts in the seats at the table and the qualifications required to take or maintain a particular seat. It is the fact that millions of Americans are reaching and exceeding financial independence long before age 65. Some are self-made entrepreneurs; others have done well with stock incentives through their employers. Some have paired their own earnings with assets inherited from parents. Each of them is facing new questions about what life can and will look like from here forward.

For the first time in history, millions of people are becoming financially independent long before society's predetermined retirement age of 65. The concept of work-until-you're-no-longer-productive-then-retire is becoming obsolete. For centuries, accumulation has been America's focal point. Now, for many people, that point has unexpectedly shifted: they have reached financial independence earlier than anticipated. If production of capital is no longer necessary, how should they spend their time? For wealth holders in this situation, money's usefulness has remained but its purpose has changed. Instead of fixating on achieving financial security, they can set their sights on opportunity and impact. Who will help them figure out what this new vantage point is all about?

Meanwhile, financial advisers are longing for deeper intimacy in client relationships. A few prized in-the-zone client relationships have sparked a hunger for the deepening of all client relationships. If you could just spend every day in that trusted adviser mode, work wouldn't feel like work at all.

There is agitation and discomfort in both camps. Wealth holders need guidance and direction and advisers are looking for a more meaningful way to operate. This is an incredible time in our industry's evolution: the simultaneous contemplations of wealth holders and their advisers can stimulate greater relationship intimacy, yet only if handled with care. Advisers must evaluate the role they wish to play among the variety of new and existing advisers the wealth holder engages. They must likewise address what behaviors will be required to earn or maintain the right to play that role and the compensation structure they must adopt to support it. We believe that without this type of intentionality, even the industry's overachievers may find themselves relegated to a place of reduced enjoyment, ego, and profit.

For decades, the financial services marketplace has perpetuated a culture that manufactured salespeople. Product manufacturers, including large institutions, relied on field forces to distribute their goods. Companies put their top producers on pedestals, at the podium at company meetings, and on stage at annual award ceremonies. The reward for transactional success came in the form of elaborate incentive trips, stock options, and cash bonuses.

This historical structure has served America well. The incentives caused high-integrity sales professionals to urge their clients to action—to protect their families with proper insurance coverage and prudent investment choices. The industry never had a reason to believe that the marketplace would one day begin to reject or question the model.

AN ERA OF AFFLUENCE

The era of affluence refers to the current point in history with regards to material wealth. It is an era in which more people are finding themselves with more money at an earlier age, and as a result, the sheer quantity of choices they face has increased exponentially. The pressure—internally and by society—to make good choices has increased on a parallel trajectory. They can send their kids to any school they wish and take any vacation they want. They can buy an education, an island, or a seat on the board.

What happens when a wealth holder consciously becomes aware that they have more financial resources than they are ever going to need? They begin to come to grips with the fact that wealth is not the end point they spent a lifetime perceiving it to be. No, wealth is merely the means to an end. Somebody moved the prize and the spot is vacant. Where should they place their daily focus? Contemplative wealth holders are beginning to see wealth as an accelerator. It is a tool for magnifying meaning and purpose in life. It provides leverage. But leverage toward what?

As wealth holders achieve this financial self-actualization, they are hit with a whole new realm and depth of questions. What is the end? What is the larger purpose of my existence? Who am I and where might I derive meaning in my daily life? How have I made a difference and how can I make a difference from here forward? Is it in the realm of personal growth, family legacy, or social capital? What is the next mountain to climb?

Meanwhile, advisers are being forced to defend and consider the structure in which they do business. Am I a salesperson or an adviser? If I'm an adviser, how am I tangibly different from the top-quality sales professional in the office next to me? Am I a fiduciary? Who do I represent? Many are confused about how they should operate. Indeed, some are a bit muddled about how they currently operate.

The contemplation is occurring on both sides of the table.

Wealth holders are questioning the traditional longstanding model of acquiring products and services, and advisers are questioning their processes for bringing services to market.

There is a point of peace amid this chaos. A solution already exists. This book was written to offer insight around how to intentionally develop your business so that it matches the needs of the market you wish to pursue. We offer several proven methodologies for adapting to wealth holders' new cravings. The opportunities vary based on the assets and mindset of the wealth holder, and the skill set and desired relationship dynamics of the adviser. Therefore, unlike any other time in the history of wealth-related services, advisers must make a conscious decision about the role they wish to play and the business structure they must build to support it, and then design a compensation structure that is congruous with both. Then and only then can they implement a long-term strategy to create it.

“If we look beyond today and into the tomorrows of our businesses, it is in that space that we might capture a glimpse of these changes taking hold and demanding action.”

OPENING THE SPACES IN OUR MINDS

It is important to acknowledge that generalizations are inherently inaccurate when measured against individual circumstances. Yet there is much to gain by analyzing a group based on common characteristics. In the pages that follow, rest assured that if you look for things that seem incongruent with your view of the industry, you will find them. As entrepreneurs, we often manage by exception in order to protect our confidence.

Yet in the privacy of our reading chairs, we can look beyond the relationships and the pieces of our worlds that currently work well. If we look beyond today and into the tomorrows of our businesses, it is in that space that we might capture a glimpse of these changes taking hold and demanding action.

EXERCISE:

Draw a horizontal line that represents a timeline of your relationship with a particular client. The left-hand-most point represents your very first interaction, perhaps many years ago. The right-hand-most point represents your final or eternal interaction with the family. Plot the achievements of the relationship on the timeline. Do these points represent transactions or new plateaus in the wealth holder's thinking? Do they affect the wealth holder and his or her family and community now or posthumously? What context has been documented to ensure clear interpretation and receipt of the structures and their intent by the recipients?

Relationship with the Jones Family

Sold term insurance to cover John's earnings at the factory	Set up college savings plan for John Jr.	John starts his own plant. Referred to estate planning attorney for wills & trusts	Convinced him to develop buy/sell agreement; company now worth $12M	Set up GST planning to get assets down to grandkids tax-free.
1985	**1989**	**1995**	**1999**	**2007**

2 *The Right Side of the Table*

CHAPTER AT A GLANCE:

For as long as there have been tables in board rooms, advisers have jockeyed for the most powerful seat at the wealth holder's planning table. We use the table as a metaphor to stimulate deeper accountability about where a particular adviser should sit based on their business model. At the table of the future, all the seats will be up for grabs, but grabbing first or tugging hardest will no longer be enough to maintain your seat.

A meeting is set. Advisers prepare. The wealth holder arrives. Everyone takes a seat and communication begins. Expectations, reactions, and decisions are all brought forth at the table. The participants surround this flat plane in a ritual of debate and communication. By nature of its shape, it carries hope of an even playing field. Yet it's a place where thought, ego, and motive can roll endlessly once in motion—little marbles of opportunity in search of their perfect resting points. The edges of the

The Table Diagram

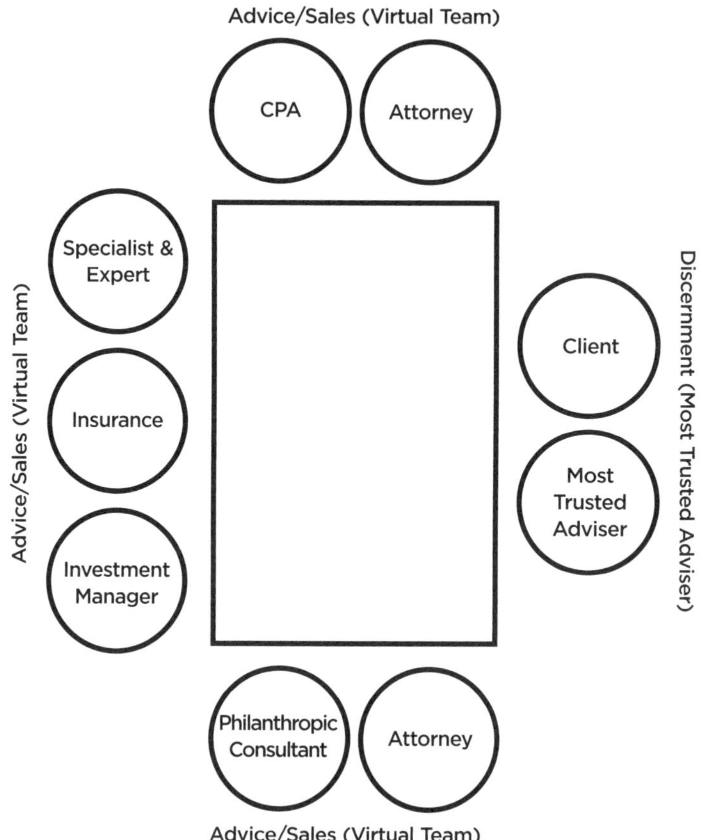

field are lined with players, each with their own marbles. Some marbles are hidden in their pockets and some are placed right there on the table for all to see. The wealth holder has a few of his own.

This is our field of commerce in the wealth holder's planning life. All of the players are important, yet how can they work as a team, each in their own best seat, so that every wealth holder feels ownership and pride when the game is over? Welcome to the proverbial table. Where would you like to sit?

When you approach something with intent, you often pull a chair

NET WORTH BRACKETS REFERENCED THROUGHOUT THIS BOOK:

Based on our personal experiences in working with wealth holders and the experiences of the thousands of advisers we have trained across the United States and Canada, we believe marketplace behaviors can be segmented into four categories:

- ***Emerging Affluent:*** *Under $1 million or $150,000 in annual household income*
- ***Affluent:*** *$1–3 million or $150,000–$250,000 in annual household income*
- ***Emerging Wealthy:*** *$3–10 million or $250,000–$500,000 in annual household income*
- ***High Wealth:*** *$10 million or more or $500,000 or more in annual household income*

Source: Paul G. Schervish, Ph.D., Director, Center on Wealth and Philanthropy, Professor of Sociology, Boston College

up to a table. Family dinners take place at tables. The White House contains dozens of elaborate tables at which diplomats and strategists gather to protect our liberty. When a wealth holder wants to consult his or her advisers about their wealth, they come to the planning table.

In society at large, we do a dance about who gets to sit where. Dad sits at the head of the table during family dinners. At weddings and galas, the seating chart is meticulously designed to keep certain people together and others apart. Somewhere in time, someone decided that how a group surrounds a table was crucial to how people communicate.

We believe the table is an excellent metaphor for how relationship dynamics will play out as planning for affluent families evolves. It offers a single, visual reference that allows us to quickly assess motives, communication styles, compensation, liability, and even industry baggage. Your seat at the table is determined by many factors. Like a multi-layered interview process, you must assess yourself in certain arenas and carry certain behavioral traits in order to fill a particular seat.

This book is about one company's vision of how the financial services industry is changing. The table metaphor illustrates who will be expected to sit in which seats under the relationship and team dynamics of the future. We can also use it to examine the wealth holder's changing cravings, preferences, and tolerances in planning and the manner in which planning ideas are served up. We can use it to stimulate conversation with our existing wealth holder clients and the teams on which we currently serve. When a wealth holder hears a caution or an opportunity, the table metaphor can help place the information in context.

THE ADVISER STYLES AND THE SEATS AT THE TABLE

As the right side of the table model becomes more prevalent, relationship and expertise will no longer be sufficient to secure your place at the table. For greater introspection about how behavioral and business traits will affect your seat going forward, review the Adviser Styles Grid in Chapter 4. It describes three key styles—the sales style, the advice style, and the discernment style—and suggests that your behaviors and financial motivations directly influence your seat at the table.

WHO GETS TO SIT WHERE

On one side of the proverbial table is the wealth holder. Directly beside him or her is the most trusted adviser. No one else is sitting on their side of the table.

On the opposite side of the table sits anyone operating in the sales style. Their compensation is based solely on transactions. This includes life insurance professionals who do not charge fees, and specialist/ experts in deep technical disciplines who earn contingent compensation only if the deal is executed. It includes property and casualty, long-term care, disability, and any other insurance providers. It also includes philanthropic advisers if they come to the table representing a particular charity.

All professionals operating in the sales style take their seats opposite the wealth holder. This does not mean their topic is adversarial;

it simply means the wealth holder wants to keep an eye on their contributions. Everyone knows they're seated at the table with a motive of commerce. For the professional seated on this side of the table, every element of their behavior must dispel the perception of questionable motives.

At the two remaining ends of the table, the rest of the core team takes their seats. These advisers operate in the advice style. They are the money managers, lawyers, and accountants who serve permanent roles on the wealth holder's team. It also includes the wealth holder's chief financial officer, trust officers, and possibly a fee-for-service financial planner who serves a role not filled by the most trusted adviser. The advice style and its accompanying location at the table offers a comfortable resting point for advisers who enjoy an implicit role of trust on the planning team yet don't wish to take on the comprehensive leadership and accountability required by the most trusted adviser.

THE TRUST FORMULA[1]

The Trust Formula, as introduced in *The Trusted Advisor*, has tremendous relevance to the right side of the table model. It allows wealth holders to evaluate trust in the context of who should sit where at their planning tables. The Trust Formula provides a measurement of accountability for trust in relationships and a structure for wealth holders to evaluate trust in their existing, often longstanding advisory relationships. It is a mathematical formula that measures the four layers of behavior that make up trust.

The Trust Formula:

$$\frac{C + R + I}{SO}$$

C = Credibility. Credibility represents accuracy and completeness. It also accounts for the ability to anticipate needs and articulate insights.

R = Reliability. Reliability represents repeated links between

promise and action. It also includes communicating in the client's preferred medium of communication, and the frequency of contact.
I = Intimacy. Intimacy represents a willingness to discuss tough topics, and the ability to do so in a manner that is palatable and even welcome.
SO = Self-orientation. Self-orientation represents anything that draws focus away from the client and toward the planner. It quantifies the adviser's underlying motivation for being in the relationship. It includes a verbal tendency to spend too much time relating the client's stories to your own stories. Note that self-orientation is the denominator and is therefore significant to the total score. It has the ability to break down successful ratings in the other elements of trust. In this category, a low score means the adviser is not self-oriented.

The Trust Formula allows advisers to rate themselves in each category based on the score they believe their clients would give them. Each category receives a score of between one and ten. When using this exercise to help a wealth holder evaluate the existing planning team, here are some questions they can use to complete the assessment:

- **Credibility:** How deep and thorough is your adviser's expertise in his or her respective area? Factors may include length of experience, education, and professional designations. It may also include their effectiveness in past engagements. How good are they at their craft?
- **Reliability:** Do your advisers do what they say? Do they keep deadlines? How does the quality of their actual work product compare to their promises? Do they show up on time for meetings and complete tasks and projects without leaving loose ends dangling?
- **Intimacy:** Are the advisers driven by emotional honesty? Are they willing to bare their own souls a bit, allowing vulnerability to be mutual? Are the advisers willing and able to expand the bounds of acceptable topics while maintaining mutual respect?
- **Self-orientation:** How confident are you that the advisers put

your interests ahead of their own? Is their presence at the table solely financially motivated, or do they have a sincere desire to achieve results for you? How does compensation structure impact motivations?

THE TRUST FORMULA AND THE SIDES OF THE TABLE

On the various sides of the table, certain aspects of the Trust Formula become particularly important. On the wealth holder's side of the table, intimacy is paramount. This is not the situational intimacy of a 20-year relationship. It requires an adviser to be incredibly skilled in the core traits of building intimacy. A key factor is the quality of discovery, or conversations, that occurs at the beginning of the relationship. We offer more on this in Chapter 4: The Three Adviser Styles.

On the ends of the table, where advisers are operating in the advice style, credibility and reliability are crucial. They are the core elements that define quality advice. In these seats, the adviser is being paid for their expertise and vantage point. The ideas and recommendations must be accurate, sound, and on time.

On the opposite side of the table, where advisers are operating in the sales style, a complete lack of self-orientation must be evident at all times. Because these seats are filled by specialists/experts who are compensated on contingency, there is a subconscious inclination to assume they are in it for themselves. They don't get paid unless their idea wins.

On the sales side of the table, as the industry evolves, clients will expect all fees and commissions to be fully disclosed. Thousands of advisers are already doing this, and you may find yourself in competition against someone who has volunteered the information to the wealth holder. Advisers will also have to justify the value of their participation in the transaction in correlation to the commission income derived. Confidence about the amount and form of your compensation is paramount. If you are at all self-conscious about it, the others at the table will sense it. It is worth noting that most trusted advisers receiving commissions for product transactions will be expected to provide equivalent disclosure.

THE PLANNING HORIZON

The single most dysfunctional element of planning for affluent families is the tendency for advisers to move too quickly into solutions—the strategies and tactics for executing a plan. What was the underlying problem? We have found that while advisers are focused on eliminating estate taxes and directing more and more money to heirs, wealth holders are more concerned about what will happen to the heirs when the money's in hand.

We operate in an industry built on the use of tools: investment vehicles, insurance products, legal documents, and tax returns. When the wealth holder shows up for planning, advisers often measure success by the quality of the technical strategy they design. Yet at the end of the planning cycle, does the wealth holder feel temporary relief that the planning cycle is over, or do they feel a lasting sense of empowerment about their vision for the use of the wealth?

A couple who has inherited substantial wealth enters a conversation with tremendous angst about the impact of the wealth on their kids. Streams of advisers pass through the door eager to take seats at the table. They toss out strategy after fantastic strategy. The couple becomes frustrated and overwhelmed. Many of the ideas appear to be logical, sound business decisions, yet no action is taken. The solutions don't feel like their solutions. They don't clearly correlate to their perspective of the problem. Everyone at the table is so preoccupied with the beauty of the solutions, they forget to notice that the wealth holders haven't decided what they really want to solve.

The Planning Horizon is a simple decision-making tool with profound impact. It offers a central point for contemplation of any difficult topic. As such, it is particularly valuable for wealth

"Everyone at the table is so preoccupied with the beauty of the solutions, they forget to notice that the wealth holders haven't decided what they really want to solve."

holders who find themselves circling through the same stressful topics over and over again without achieving the satisfaction of forward progress.

The Planning Horizon represents a metaphoric horizontal line. Conversations that take place *above the horizon* surround the wealth holder's deepest and most personal intent for their wealth. Why are they planning in the first place? Conversations that take place *below the horizon* surround the strategies and products that can influence the achievement of the wealth holder's goals as identified *above the horizon*.

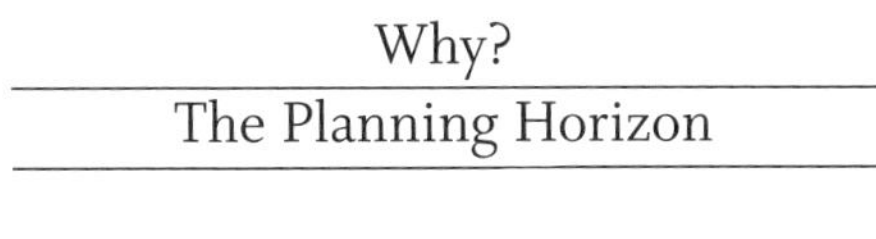

The couple described above came to the proverbial table to work on their planning. They're terrified that the wealth will rob their kids of purpose, drive, or work ethic. What could possibly be done to protect against this? These questions are screaming for a thoughtful conversation above the horizon. Instead, they were answered with solutions below the horizon. We can put the money in trust. The trustee will carefully scrutinize every withdrawal. They'll only get a match on their current salary. They won't get the money until age 30, 35, or 40.

An above-the-line conversation uses authentic discernment-based communication, thereby progressing altogether differently:

- What are you afraid of?
- What makes you fearful about that?
- Why is that?
- What would be your ultimate *positive* goal for how the wealth could enhance the lives of your kids?

Through six or seven levels of questioning, the wealth holders arrive at a self-stimulated ah-ha. They understand what they want to achieve surrounding the on-the-streets impact of the wealth on their kids. The most trusted adviser now documents the thinking in writing and reviews it with the wealth holder. Once it is confirmed to be accurate and fully reflective of their goals, the advisory team comes together at the planning table. The couple's intent is shared with the advisory team who is then chartered to make it come to life using planning strategies.

Acknowledging that the ultimate underlying desires of the wealth holder are never found below the horizon is the power of the Planning Horizon. Proper discovery above the horizon leads to effective solutions below the horizon. Einstein said that true creativity

ADVISER STORY: ***Note—For all stories included in this book, the names of the wealth holders have been changed.***

Chuck Ebersole, of Foord, Van Bruggen, Ebersole & Pajak in Sacramento, California, helped a client think more clearly using the Planning Horizon to facilitate their conversations.

> *My client was 77 at the time and was worth $30 million. He was referred to me by his attorney for some investment advice regarding his profit-sharing rollover to an IRA. When we met, I told him I worked in a different way and wanted to show him how I approached planning. I began to explain the philosophy behind the Planning Horizon and drew out the diagram on a plain sheet of paper. I explained that traditional planning takes people below the line too soon, suggesting fancy strategies before there's consensus about the vision the strategies are supposed to support.*
>
> *His posture began to change and he seemed to relax a bit. I think his guard went down because he sensed a solution to a problem he hadn't been able to put his finger on. Even though he had great advisers, there was no master vision driving his planning.*

[Continued on Page 21]

[Continued from Page 20]

We talked about the fact that most successful wealth holders find themselves with a variety of strategies in place that were brought to them by different advisers at different times. He became very engaged in the conversation and voiced a concern that no one had a good handle on his overall plan, not even him. He admitted that his plan lacked vision and therefore wasn't a real plan, but rather a composite of fragments.

He was very curious about the possibility of having someone help clarify his broader vision for his wealth, and then coordinate all of his advisers using his vision to search out relevant strategies and tools. No one had ever offered to do that for him before. Plenty of people wanted to work with him below the line, but no one wanted to take charge of helping him design his legacy in nonfinancial terms first. He hired me to take him through a planning process using the Planning Horizon and the deeper questioning utilized in the discernment style. He made all of these decisions prior to discussing what he came in for in the first place, his $1 million rollover, and he left my office pleased and relieved.

is in problem formation. He believed that if the hypothesis lacked truth or clarity, the science deployed to prove it was useless. If you're running around looking for the solution on your client's behalf, and they don't seem all that interested, take a step back in planning. Ask yourself, "What is the true problem at hand?" What does the wealth holder think the problem is? Who defined it—you or them? Be careful not to stop at the first or most superficial answer—in your mind or in theirs.

THE PLANNING HORIZON AND THE SEATS AT THE TABLE

The Planning Horizon directly correlates to the dynamic that plays out at the wealth holder's planning table. Forward progress requires clarity. Clarity requires trust. Trust earns an adviser the right to sit at the table. When the ideas shared at the planning table solve a problem unique to the wealth holder's thinking, he or she will confidently engage in consideration and execution.

THE UTOPIAN TABLE OF THE FUTURE

For so long the industry has taught young salespeople to grab a strategic seat at the table. The corner represents greater intimacy. The facing side represents opposition. Taking the right seat moves you upstream. It raises your stature. Our work in this arena has revealed a shift in control. At the table of the future, the seats will be clearly defined by the wealth holder and the adviser will have to earn his or her right to take a particular place.

EXERCISE:

Use the Trust Formula to rate how you are perceived by your best relationships. Remember that for successful advisers, the ability to achieve greater success or satisfaction from their businesses requires introspection around the finest details of execution. When you're doing 98 percent of things right, you have to dig deeper into your psyche and your pattern to work on that last 2 percent.

Draw a grid on a piece of paper. Down the left side, list five great personal or professional relationships and five that are poor or not as strong. Across the top, make columns for each of the four elements of the Trust Formula. Now rate each relationship in each category. Move down the columns, not across. Remember to score yourself as you believe the relationship would score you, not as you feel you perform. Be especially honest about your scores in self-orientation. Low self-orientation scores show that you're in the relationship to give something. High self-orientation scores show you're in the relationship to take something. Most relationships involve both. The goal is to identify the primary orientation.

ENDNOTE

1. David H. Maister, Charles H. Green and Robert M. Galford. *The Trusted Advisor*, Free Press 2000. Used with written permission.

3 *The Chairs Are Changing*

CHAPTER AT A GLANCE:

Decades ago, getting financial advice was easy for the consumer. Roles were clear, life was simple, and for most people, one or two advisers could handle all their needs. Now there are more people with more money, and at younger ages. As financial complexity set in, demand for services followed. Meanwhile, advisers' roles have morphed and expanded. As a result, the industry is at a crossroads of consumer perception. The chairs at the proverbial conference room table will be filled with advisers who adapt to changing times. Here is a brief look at how to navigate your place in the evolution.

When life was simple and the middle class was the largest facet of our economic makeup, we could easily make it through our time on earth with a single adviser or two. Insurance people sold insurance, accountants gave tax advice, and lawyers drafted wills. Decades ago, it was the rare wealthy family that needed five to ten different types of advisers over the course of their lifetimes. Today the quantity and diversity of issues that would warrant such a team is not so uncommon.

The increase in quantity and complexity of choice for the wealth holder has paved the way for new business models and career choices for financial advisers. Historically, the financial services engine was driven by large companies that manufactured products. The industry evolved not as a profession but as a distribution channel. Salespeople brought the products to market and were paid if the sale was consummated. The acquisition process was clear to both buyer and seller.

For those of us who've been in the industry for decades, we cut our teeth selling products. Perhaps over time, we acquired wisdom and knowledge about creative ways to use the products and shared this with our clients and prospects. But at the end of the day, we were operating in *the sales style.*

Some professionals were so adept at selling and achieved such great success they earned autonomy from the manufacturer. Either their sales managers acknowledged their success and left them to operate with little supervision, or they branched off into an independent structure in which they could represent the products of many manufacturers. On paper, this increased the wealth holder's choices, but the choices weren't always presented to them front and center.

In the 1970s, some advisers began to crave greater context for their roles in clients' lives. They knew their work was important, but it felt transactional, somewhat empty. This stimulated some to evolve into a planning mode of doing business. What was once financial services—the delivery of products—gave way to financial planning, the delivery of advice, education, wisdom, and knowledge. In the 1990s, some began to attach a fee-for-advice model to the planning portion of their work. Hence *the advice style* was born.

Today, we have found that advisers' behaviors have naturally pooled into three modus operandi: the sales style, the advice style, and the discernment style, which are introduced on the following pages. Inherent to each method is the vantage point, communication style, and revenue model of the adviser.

THE THREE ADVISER STYLES

These styles offer insight into advisers' varying roles and behaviors within those roles. They also offer decision-making opportunities regarding current and future business models.

- *The sales style: Persuading a prospect or client to follow a specific course of action or purchase a particular product.*
- *The advice style: Providing an opinion about how to remedy or enhance a particular situation.*
- *The discernment style: Asking a sufficient number of the right questions for consumers to achieve their own conclusions.*

THE SALES STYLE

We believe that much of the industry operates in the sales style, where incentive-based compensation is their primary revenue driver. This style is based on persuading clients to follow a specific course of action or to purchase a particular product. Clients need life insurance to protect their estate tax liability. They need nontraditional investments to protect their downside risk.

Our experience indicates that this style works well in the emerging-affluent market (under $1 million) because the wealth holder may not tolerate the longer sales cycle inherent in planning, or a fee-for-advice compensation structure.

IS THE SALES STYLE RIGHT FOR YOU?

If the majority of your revenue comes from incentive-based compensation, you are operating in the sales style. The sales style represents an important seat at the wealth holder's planning table. It is ideal for professionals who enjoy developing deep expertise in a particular technical discipline, and who prefer not to be accountable for developing and implementing multidisciplinary plans for wealth holders.

THE ADVICE STYLE

We believe that another substantial portion of the industry is operating somewhere between the sales style and the advice style. The latter is a style in which the adviser gathers data and provides an opinion about what could or should be done to remedy or enhance a particular situation. The advice style is focused on clearly articulating the client's best course of action as seen through the adviser's insight, expertise, and experience.

The advice style has been proven effective in the affluent market ($1 to $3 million of net worth) and emerging-wealthy ($3 to $10 million) markets. These sectors have generally demonstrated a willingness to pay a fee for planning services. However, they may prefer to get in and out of the cycle quickly, and therefore value the delivery of recommendations they can accept or decline.

Many advisers will quickly slip themselves into the advice style category. They offer planning, therefore they are advisers. In reality, many professionals who are creating financial plans are actually operating in the sales style. The distinction is in the compensation drivers, the planning and communications methodologies, and the professional's primary underlying commerce goal in the relationship.

Some advisers are currently applying the advice style to a higher-end marketplace, and, on reading this, may question our $10 million cap. Our experience indicates that its acceptance by wealth holders worth $10 million or more is decreasing and that the rate of decline will quicken.

IS THE ADVICE STYLE RIGHT FOR YOU?

For those who currently provide planning services and charge planning fees, it is possible that you are operating in the advice style. In this realm, it is primarily the wealth holder's hard data—assets, tax liability, and distributions to heirs—that the planning embraces.

THE DISCERNMENT STYLE

We believe that less than one-tenth of 1 percent of the industry is

> "Most advisers ask questions. Some advisers ask follow-up questions. The discernment-based adviser asks enough of the right questions for the wealth holder to reach their own conclusions at far greater depth than they could through the delivery of external recommendations."

currently operating in the discernment style—perhaps only 100 advisers nationally. The discernment style is based on the belief that if you ask your clients enough of the right questions, they will come to substantial conclusions about the overarching vision for the use of their wealth. This goes beyond legal documents that indicate how the wealth should be distributed and when. It documents their intent for how the wealth can enhance the lives of the family members.

Through our decades of training and coaching advisers working in the upper net worth brackets, we have seen increased demand for the discernment style in the emerging-wealthy market ($3 to 10 million) and we believe it will rapidly become the most accepted style in the high-wealth market ($10 million+). These wealth holders do not want to be sold or told. They want facts, but they prefer facilitation of their decision making over flat do-or-die recommendations. The only current obstacle they face in adopting this style of planning is that they haven't yet come across the opportunity.

Most advisers ask questions. Some advisers ask follow-up questions. The discernment-based adviser asks enough of the right questions for the wealth holder to reach his or her own conclusions at far greater depth than they could through the delivery of external recommendations.

IS THE DISCERNMENT STYLE RIGHT FOR YOU?

When an adviser begins to search for the same kind of deep introspection that a wealth holder longs for in his or her planning life, the two minds merge at the discernment style. In this style, the adviser uses deeper and deeper questioning to stimulate the client to reach his or her own best conclusions.

ADVISER STORY PROVIDED BY SCOTT FITHIAN

I first met my client, Diane, in the early 1990s, when I was doing planning for her husband, Joe. He was very successful in the home-building business and she had raised their four children. Typical of many marriages of this era (Joe and Diane were in their fifties), Joe was making many of the financial decisions and Diane wasn't very involved. At that time in my practice, I was operating in the advice style while developing and testing my discernment-based behaviors. It worked in the sense that we implemented some great strategies for Joe, yet there were two things that just didn't feel right to me: Diane's lack of involvement in the planning, and the fact that I couldn't get Joe to go deeper into developing his broader vision for the wealth. In 2003, Joe died rather suddenly at the young age of 62. Diane was shocked, grief stricken, and financially paralyzed. She felt disconnected from the $25 million she now owned—like the wealth wasn't hers.

Over the next three years, I had the opportunity to become one of Diane's closest friends and her primary adviser. We had many heart-to-heart conversations in which it felt like time was standing still for both of us. I wasn't thinking about what she needed to do and she was in no condition to make any buying decisions, or to make any substantial changes in her estate.

In our relationship, I applied the discernment style wholeheartedly. I posed stimulating questions and she surprised herself with her answers. Each layer of questioning created deeper clarity for her regarding who she could be in relation to the wealth. She began to develop a sense of herself as the 62-year-old owner of $25 million who had all the passion and influence to accomplish great things. She became extremely philanthropic and embraced her next phase of life in an entirely new context. I know that Diane would have never achieved all of this without the application of the discernment style.

AN OPPORTUNITY TO IMPROVE WEALTH HOLDERS' RESULTS

More detail on the three adviser styles is presented in Chapter 4 and throughout this book. The basic premise is this: if you're craving greater intimacy during your conversations with wealth holders, discernment-based communication is a way to achieve it. If you sincerely wish that more individuals and families of significant wealth would take comprehensive action to establish their legacies and protect their families, discernment-based communication offers a proven solution. However, it is not a secret bullet to increase product sales. It is a specific tool for increasing wealth holders' clarity about the ultimate intent for their tangible and intangible assets.

Advisers can fully embrace discernment-based communication as a business model and become a most trusted adviser, or you can increase client intimacy and therefore the quality and depth of the wealth holder's decision making by incorporating these behaviors into your existing sales style or advice style of interaction. Sample questions are offered in subsequent chapters.

THE POWER AND CONSEQUENCE OF CHOICE

The broadening of the marketplace brings with it the luxury of choice. It creates space for every type of adviser to build a preferred business model. With choice comes consequence. This book helps advisers anticipate their futures, lending insight into the evolution in wealth holders' thinking, to what they crave and tolerate, so that advisers can make educated decisions about what their future businesses might look like.

Ambiguity in your business model shows up as confusion to your prospects. Some professionals find themselves with decreased sales effectiveness, yet they haven't quite become an adviser. Cash flow suffers. Until you come to terms with your own best fit, it's difficult to perfect your craft.

Professionals who wish to move upmarket and currently operate in the sales style may hit obstacles during their journey. Salespeople who crave the professional cachet of operating as an adviser, but have never left their sales roots and behaviors, must embrace a wholesale shift in how they operate. For some, this means learning how to ask for planning fees and how to structure a fee-for-advice practice while perhaps still credibly collecting product commissions.

For those who currently provide planning services and charge planning fees, it is possible that you are operating in the advice style. In this realm, it is primarily the wealth holder's hard data—assets, tax liability, and distributions to heirs—that the planning embraces. Reputable, well-equipped professionals operating in the advice style fill a great void for the wealth holder. Often, the breadth of their vantage point is greater than the sales professional. This allows them to spot and fix problems that professionals operating in a single core discipline aren't motivated or trained to address.

When an adviser begins to search for the same kind of deep introspection that a wealth holder longs for in his or her planning life, the two minds merge at the discernment style. For those who believe they were born to operate in the discernment style, the traditional industry channels aren't supporting their evolution. Indeed, this is new thinking. But it is rooted in the natural hierarchy of the way our psyches are programmed to make decisions. When one's fundamental financial needs are met, it frees the mind to ponder other types of existence. That free-thinking space in our brains longs to be fed with innovation and new ways of problem solving.

How do you engage in these conversations with wealth holders? How do you facilitate their craving for greater meaning and purpose through use of their material assets? How do you charge for the services? No technical or sales conference can prepare you to succeed in this realm.

What lies ahead for every adviser is simply an intentional choice. If you choose to operate in the sales style or the advice style with wealth holders worth $3 to $10 million or more, take notice of their changing reactions toward your existing business structure. If you choose to operate in the discernment style, be certain you have the raw ability and desire the substantial responsibility you are about to embrace on behalf of your clients. Compensation structure and fiduciary responsibility are just the starting points. Whichever you choose, planning to be ahead of the curve always lends greater opportunity for a wise choice.

4 The Three Adviser Styles

CHAPTER AT A GLANCE:

Changes in consumer behavior and the financial services industry have caused professionals to naturally gravitate into three different operating modes—the sales style, the advice style, and the discernment style. Each style represents behavior traits and insights into how advisers frame their prospecting opportunities and client relationships. The styles can reveal barriers, stigmas, and opportunities in current behavior patterns, and how these correlate to or conflict with an adviser's desired marketplace or business model.

This chapter delves deeper into each of the adviser styles. It offers an opportunity to embrace and understand the wealth holder's changing cravings, tolerances, and needs. While our experience indicates there are three distinct business and behavior styles, practically speaking, many advisers operate in more than one style. Consider, for example, a partner in a law firm who designs advanced estate planning strategies, yet is directly compensated for the volume of business she brings into the firm. She is operating in the sales style and the advice style, and perhaps the discernment style as well. The goal of this book is to increase advisers' awareness of how they're communicating with clients, and how their communication styles complement or hinder their service models.

THE SALES STYLE

The dictionary definition of "sell" is "to persuade another to recognize the worth or desirability of something." The sales style is based on persuading the client to follow a specific course of action or to purchase a specific product or service.

The sales style is effective as long as everyone understands the rules of the game. This means full disclosure about how you get paid and what services you're providing. In financial services, there are salespeople who do great work, ask great questions, and obtain the necessary facts to determine suitability of the products they're selling.

However, there are also many advisers operating in the sales style who use professional titles to suggest they're providing more than product solutions. Without offering a thorough planning process, a simple investment or retirement projection is provided. The consumer thinks he or she has done planning.

All of the seats at the advisory table must be filled by experts who care, and the sales role is an important role. However, in an industry that dances across the television and newsstands with smoke and mirrors, advisers owe it to wealth holders to articulate the nature and depth of our particular role. Consider your last home-buying experi-

ADVISERS WHO THRIVE IN THE SALES STYLE

- *Enjoy the thrill of the kill*
- *Lose interest or momentum after the initial sale*
- *Love to learn the intricacies of how powerful products work*
- *Enjoy the simplicity of a transactional business*

ence. Perhaps you had an extremely positive experience with the sales professional you worked with, even actively referred him or her to others. Everyone at the buying table knew their purpose. The flow of compensation was clearly disclosed.

APPLYING MODEL TO MARKETPLACE

In the emerging-affluent market, the sales style not only works well, but it is the most financially feasible style. Consumers here are willing to take the baseline risk of working with someone who hopes to complete a transaction as remuneration for their investment in the relationship. They accept the underlying transactional dynamic in exchange for not having to pay a planning fee.

While recognizing the feasibility of this style in the emerging-affluent sector, we must likewise acknowledge the changing flavor of the industry as a whole. As many advisers move their businesses up the wealth spectrum, the viability of the sales style comes into question. Why are advisers picking elaborate professional titles and obtaining professional designations at record rates? Consumers are changing. Their tolerance for pure persuasion is waning. They are dictating a different business style going forward.

As you move into the affluent market, wealth holders are less and less willing to risk making financial decisions through a salesperson. Even if they like and trust you, they know your best days are those in which you make a sale. And there's always the chance that from two good options, you'll make a stronger recommendation for the one that derives a greater commission or company incentive.

In the affluent market, professionals operating in the sales style will increasingly find another member of the wealth holder's team directly involved in decision making. You can still effectively prospect to and build relationships directly with wealth holders, but they are likely to obtain the opinion of their CPA or attorney during the process. Our experience indicates that if you wish to continue working in the $3 million or more marketplace and operate in the sales style, it is paramount to sharpen your skill set for aligning with and not alienating the existing members of the advisory team.

Also, as affluent wealth holders seek the opinions of their other team members, those team members quickly see the light bulb of opportunity inherent in bringing their own best choice to the team table. They control the access points and possibly get paid on the deals. Attorneys, CPAs, and other professionals must understand your worth so they will consider saving a seat for you at the table.

In the emerging-wealthy and high-wealth markets, the days of a wealth holder maintaining a 20-year friendship with their life insurance guy and making buying decisions directly with that person are quickly evaporating. These wealth holders are beginning to rely on the independent advice of a professional other than the salesperson to make their ultimate decisions. Relationship will no longer supersede the buyer's due diligence. The salesperson will be an important member of the team, but the product acquisition will take place through the most trusted adviser as a filter.

THE ADVICE STYLE

Advice is defined as an "opinion about what could be done about a situation or problem." The advice style is focused on clearly articulating the best course of action based on the adviser's insight, perspective, and experience.

In an effort to move upmarket and adapt to the needs of affluent wealth holders, many advisers have naturally migrated away from a sales-only style of doing business toward an advice-based style. The advice style works well in the affluent market segment where the financial decisions are still fairly straightforward. The wealth holder wants to enlist expertise and understands the structural relationship options available to them. They are becoming increasingly amenable to paying a separate financial planning fee for professional advice. In turn, they expect a real plan and established systems and processes for execution. There is tremendous fee-for-value opportunity for advisers operating in the advice style in the affluent marketplace.

Financial advisers planning to move into or remain in this style should consider their technical knowledge, educational pedigrees, and professional designations as paramount to their success. You will increasingly be judged on your ability to provide bulletproof recommendations. Our experience indicates that the most trusted adviser of the future will have the relationship power and the obligation to drill deep into your ideas and your presentations. Those who continue to excel in the advice style will rise to this occasion by having sufficient depth of expertise to survive this key adviser's due diligence, thereby earning and retaining their seat at the table.

ADVISERS WHO THRIVE IN THE ADVICE STYLE

- *Provide value through deep technical expertise in a particular discipline*
- *Thrive on staying technically current and even designing new strategies*
- *Enjoy trust and intimacy in client relationships as they apply to executing advice, but do not wish to spend hours and hours delving into the softer side of a client's vision*

The advice style has very specific implications for advisers who wish to work in the emerging-wealthy and high-wealth marketplace. These wealth holders are more interested in a blank-slate conversation than a presentation of recommendations. They want someone who can empower them to make their own decisions, someone who is better at asking questions than suggesting solutions. They care more about the quality of the communication in the relationship than your ability to produce a highly technical financial plan. They know that technical recommendations are simply a commodity that can be purchased on the open market—a buyer's market. In the emerging-wealthy and high-wealth markets, the most trusted adviser of the future will operate in the discernment style.

THE DISCERNMENT STYLE

"Discern" is defined as "to perceive with the eyes or intellect; to detect; to recognize or comprehend mentally." Over the past several years, a new adviser style has begun to emerge surrounding the concept of discernment. The discernment style represents a communication methodology emanating from an entirely different vantage point. It is based on the fundamental belief that when it comes to creating a vision for his or her wealth, the client possesses all of his or her own best answers. They simply need the right questions and a compassionate listener.

The discernment style is least effective in the emerging-affluent and affluent segments as it requires a greater investment of time, effort, and resources than the sales style and the advice style, and wealth holders in the first two realms of affluence don't see a justifiable return on investment.

The discernment style evolved from on-the-street experiences demonstrating that in the emerging-wealthy and high-wealth markets, wealth holders do not wish to be sold on a particular solution or told to consider a certain recommendation. They are not looking for an instructor, they are looking for a guide, someone who can open doorways and expand perspective without the underlying driver of leadership or judgment. They are looking for someone who can help them see possibilities outside of their own thinking.

Good advisers ask questions. Great advisers operating in the advice style ask follow-up questions. In discernment, the advisers ask enough of the right questions for the wealth holder to arrive at his or her own ah-has. Lines of questioning have no driver except client clarity. Advisers aren't sifting through courses of action in their minds. Their only agenda item is to help the wealth holder get to a deeper level of insight.

In discernment-based planning, it's not whether the client breaks down in tears or shares a sacred story that matters. It's what you do next. Just at the point of awkwardness that makes most people want to retreat to safer ground, the discernment-based adviser steps into that space and, with permission, delves deeper. He or she takes the risk with the wealth holder that there might really be something there, a wise choice bobbing about beneath the tears.

Follow-up questions might include:

- Tell me more about that.
- What did you think about when it was happening?
- How did you feel at the time it happened?
- How do you feel now?
- How has it influenced your thinking or actions over the years?
- What major life themes emerged from that experience?
- When was the last time you spoke with someone about this?

The discernment adviser asks four, five, even six levels of questions on the same tough topic. With the context of the experience now at surface level, the point of thought offers new insight for the wealth holder and the adviser. These insights are then woven into the fabric of planning.

In the advice style, a client may tell you he or she lost a child years ago. In the discernment style, the client is likely to unearth how the event has changed him or her as a person, how it has impacted every cell of his or her being every day since it occurred.

ADVISERS WHO THRIVE IN THE DISCERNMENT STYLE

- *Can put their egos aside in favor of progress for the wealth holder, even if it means giving another team member the limelight*
- *Feel most in their zone during the intimate, coaching-type conversations they have with clients*
- *Feel that establishing a client's mission, vision, values, and goals is a powerful part of the planning process—not a cog in the wheel toward a transaction*
- *Are comfortable asking tough questions without knowing what the answer might bring*
- *May wish to use their discernment-based behaviors in a most trusted adviser role, or may prefer to operate in a single core discipline*

The discernment style is rooted in our experience that the emerging-wealthy and high-wealth markets desire a greater voice in the process. They will pay professionals to bring questions, information, and wisdom to the table. They want help gaining insight so that their own best choice rises to the surface.

The crucial difference between presenting facts and recommending what course of action to take is central to the discernment style. Consider the planning experiences you may have had in which you presented a great set of recommendations and the wealth holder never took action. In essence, the wealth holder was asked to consider your ideas and pick one.

Now consider the mindset of self-made people. They bring wisdom and often entrepreneurship to the planning table. They have made countless great decisions and at least several bad ones. They define life by their DNA-based ability to make wise choices. Then, they enter planning to find a team of experts presenting recommendations at them. Watch them back away from the table. They want to participate in the figuring-out part. Many advisers don't have a process for allowing the wealth holder to do this. The discernment style does not suggest that wealth holders want to learn how the watch is made. They want to discern whether a watch is the right solution to the right problem.

Some advisers believe that the wealth holder of today doesn't have time to engage in this style of planning, that they want to get in and out of the process as fast as possible. It is true that some wealth holders don't want to go deep. Some aren't ready and some resist the intimacy necessary to effectively plan at the discernment level. Society has taught us to content ourselves with pat answers instead of exploring the root of our discomfort and really resolving it. As a result, advisers oblige by implementing planning that serves intermediate ends—Band-Aid decisions that only account for the halfway point in the wealth holder's thinking.

Have you ever noticed that most engagements in which a client starts off wanting to get the work done quickly rarely move into implementation? Wealth holders profess a lack of time and advisers fall in step working quickly through the process. Then the backing away occurs. The wealth holder craves resolution but they're too smart to take action unless it represents a wise choice. By offering these families a true discernment opportunity, you can help emerging-wealthy and high-wealth families finally begin to feel good about their planning, making more confident and substantive progress than ever before.

MEASURING CLIENT INTIMACY

When clients cry in an adviser's presence or bare a secret they've never revealed before, some advisers seem to wear it as a badge of honor—"the wife cried at the first meeting." People cry for a wide variety of reasons—intense fear, joy, forgiveness, or a release of tension. Crying in someone's presence doesn't equate to the existence or sustainability of client intimacy. If you strive to operate in the discernment style, ask yourself the last time a client had a new and substantial ah-ha in your presence; an ah-ha about a past experience, not about your advice.

ADVISER STORY:

Tim Belber, owner of Family Wealth Services Group in Denver, Colorado, describes a breakthrough in a client's thinking that was achieved using the discernment style. The client was a self-made 60-year-old man with a net worth of $16 million. Two of his three sons worked in their blue-collar business.

"Tom called one day and said he needed to make some changes to his estate plan. There were problems with his son, Tommy Jr. It seems Tommy had begun complaining about superficial things including their office space—it wasn't fancy enough, they needed a better location, something more professional and higher profile. Tom Sr. was concerned that Tommy was financially irresponsible, that he might blow all of the assets of the business on superficial things. When we sat down to talk, I asked him what was happening in Tommy's life. It turned out he had a new wife who was a young attorney. He had started feeling peer pressure for working in an

[Continued on Page 40]

[Continued from Page 39]

industry that didn't have much cocktail-party appeal. He was reaching for ways to erase his embarrassment. By the end of our conversation, Tom Sr. realized that Tommy's behavior had nothing to do with financial irresponsibility. He needed the freedom to go out in the world—to experience having a boss that wasn't his father, to build a career with white-collar cachet.

Following Tom Sr.'s ah-ha, father and son were able to communicate openly about Tommy Jr.'s craving to experience a career outside the family business. Tom Sr. gave his full emotional support for Tommy's pursuits, and was able to constructively communicate the situation to his other son who was working in the business.

Nine months later, Tommy Jr. asked to return and work in the family business. Tom Sr. accepted. A short four months later, Tom Sr. died suddenly. Today, nearly ten years later, the two sons are running the business together. They complement each others' talents and have doubled the size of the business. If Tom Sr.'s phone call to me was followed by an appointment to change his legal documents, instead of a stimulated dialogue about the root problem, I firmly believe things would have turned out altogether differently."

CONTEMPLATION MEETS ACTION

When we talk about the evolution in consumer thinking described in earlier chapters, it's important to consider that the changes occurring in the wealth holder's mind are more about humanity than money. These changes are taking hold of our society at large. People are craving greater contemplation and reflection when making their most important life decisions. In the high-end financial services marketplace, every consumer wants to be truly heard by their adviser. If you're operating in the sales style or the advice style, consider incorporating discernment-based behaviors into your relationships. Consider the respect it demonstrates to your clients and the quality of interactions you can achieve through honing your skills.

Discernment-based behavior is listening without looking for a solution. It's asking questions that aren't designed to lead the client to a purchase. It's about helping the client still his or her world for a moment, creating a timeless space in which he or she can make a deeply confident choice.

If you choose to operate in the sales style, consider the level and type of discovery or questioning you're bringing to the client's experience. Use every sales encounter to sharpen your discovery skills. Ask questions beyond what surrounds the sale at hand. Instead of using the sale-closing questions of the past, try some discernment-based questions.

- On a scale of one to ten, how would you measure your confidence level about the path we're taking?
- What is your gut telling you about what we're doing?
- How does the work we've done so far compare to the expectations you had when you first engaged us?
- Do you have any questions about the work we're doing?

"Discernment-based behavior is listening without looking for a solution. It's asking questions that aren't designed to lead the client to a purchase. It's about helping the client still his or her world for a moment, creating a timeless space in which he or she can make a deeply confident choice."

As incentive-based professionals, advisers were initially trained to minimize conversation, secure the transaction, and get out. Today's consumer is savvier than that. Demonstrate your sincere interest in his or her well-being through a willingness to dwell in the decision-making process just a bit longer. Confirm that the path the wealth holder is on is not just a good path for anyone, but his or her own personal true north.

MAKE YOUR OWN BEST CHOICE

At the end of the day, what each of us faces is simply an obligation to our clients to make our own best choice. If you are a born salesperson, sell with integrity and introspection about your client's place in the world. If you enjoy being an expert in a technical discipline, delve deeper into your capabilities, expand your inventory of knowledge, and plant yourself firmly in the advice style. If you are stimulated by the depth of conversation and responsibility inherent in the discernment style, make a commitment to sharpen your skills and to operate there with the kind of intentionality inherent in being a student of your craft.

5 Choosing the Right Chair

CHAPTER AT A GLANCE:

Consumer confusion is a growing obstacle in financial services. Wealth holders lack clarity about the role their advisers play, and, as a result, often inaccurately believe their planning to be complete. For example, a successful executive worth $20 million who works with an investment manager may believe her affairs are in order, unaware of the need for in-depth financial or retirement planning. If advisers increase their own clarity about the services they offer and the style in which they operate, it can help their prospects and clients understand and fill in the missing pieces. This chapter suggests that every adviser intentionally evaluate his or her natural skill set, and then consider any new skill sets or alterations of the business model that can help you achieve your goals going forward.

Decades ago, when professionals called themselves life insurance agents and stockbrokers, consumers understood what they were buying. In the new millennium, salespeople are calling themselves coaches and everyone, regardless of product or service, seems to be a financial planner. We see new faces popping up daily, equipped only with a list of the wealthiest people they know and passing scores on several exams. It takes more planning, education, and on-the-job training to become a plumber. Still wet behind the ears, these new additions to our industry print "financial representative" on a business card and hit the streets. What are they representing? Likewise, we must consider seasoned professionals who have started to delve into new service areas. What new skill sets are required? Is the adviser fully equipped to play this new role? Was the decision financially motivated, or was it stimulated by a clear match between the wealth holders' needs and the adviser's natural talent?

CHOOSING YOUR OWN BEST CHAIR AT THE TABLE:
Clarity regarding your business model will show up as clarity for your clients and prospects. It will simplify their buying decisions and allow business to flow more smoothly. Consider the Adviser Styles Grid later in this chapter and these questions, when contemplating your seat:

- *What part of the business do you love the most?*
- *Which segments of the sales or planning cycles are the most stimulating or motivating?*
- *Where do you lose momentum or interest?*
- *What is the most common accolade you receive from clients?*
- *Picture the proverbial conference room table. Do you want to be there with the wealth holder at every meeting, or only those that pertain to your core discipline?*
- *At the planning table of the future, the seat next to the wealth holder takes on a role of confidante with accountability for every aspect of the planning. The advisers seated at the ends and opposite side are relied on for their expertise in a core discipline. Where do you see yourself sitting?*

As financial professionals, we owe it to our clients to be stewards of the relationship we've created. The plans and products a wealth holder takes home become the celebrations or the indictments that define our industry in the press and in consumers' minds—and these collectively affect our ability to do business.

RISING TO YOUR OWN OCCASION

Industry pressure has pushed many advisers into an identity crisis. With one foot in the sales style and one foot in the advice style, they're constantly straddling multiple stories and conflicting or ill-equipped compensation models. All too frequently, advisers make decisions about what to say or how to charge as they're walking down to the conference room to greet a new prospect. Sometimes the decision comes 45 minutes into the actual encounter. If you're confused, how do you think the wealth holder is feeling?

Every adviser has a natural inclination that determines his or her behavior in particular situations. In the same way, we each have new attributes to which we aspire. Understanding your true natural style offers opportunity and confidence. How were you born to operate? A person's natural disposition reveals itself under stress and pressure.

We have outlined advisers' common behaviors into 28 attributes within the three styles (the sales style, the advice style, and the discernment style). The motivation for creating this grid was to provide advisers with an opportunity for foresight and intentionality in their evolving business models. Consider how you present yourself in conversation and in your marketing literature. Is it consistent? Is it accurate? Is it a fair representation of your value proposition?

We spend our careers being told we must do certain things to survive. As entrepreneurs, it's time we reclaimed the power inherent in our choices. Our hope is that every adviser reading this book will make a firm commitment to the style in which he or she plans to operate five years from now. It may be a matter of perfecting your current style or fully stepping into a role in which you've just begun to experiment. Regardless, what training, mentoring, technology, or back-office talent and processes are required to serve your market well?

Adviser Styles Grid

Although all advisers relate to some elements of each style, each is predisposed to one style.

Style Attributes

	Sales Model	Advice Model	Discernment Model
1	Sell	Tell	Listen
2	Commodity	Service	Unique Experience
3	Self-Oriented	Credibility/Reliability	Intimacy
4	Salesmen	Technician	Generalist
5	Task	Planning	Management
6	Team Evasion	Team Participation	Team Leadership
7	Guarded	Trusted	Most Trusted
8	Income Earner	Business Manager	Business Owner
9	Solicitous	Consultative	Reflective
10	Fatal Alternative	Options	Single Best Solution
11	Sales Proposition	Planning Proposition	Value Proposition
12	Transaction-Oriented	Fee-Oriented	Relationship-Oriented
13	Client Quantity	Client Continuity	Client Quality
14	Fear	Responsibility	Inspiration
15	Product	Information	Wisdom
16	Solution Superiority	Objective Process	Client Intimacy
17	Give Away Value	Sell Advice	Paid for Wisdom
18	Product-Based Compensation	Product-Based Fee	Results-Based Fee
19	Happenstance	Planning Process	Turnkey System
20	Tactical	Comprehensive	Strategic
21	Handoff	Delegation	Integrated Team
22	Paid Per Transaction	Paid Per Plan	Paid Per Relationship
23	Short-Term Focus	Annual Focus	Lifetime Focus
24	Minimize Liberty	Overcome Liberty	Maximize Liberty
25	No Insight	Adviser Insight	Client Insight
26	Minimize Contact	Maintain Contact	Maximize Contact
27	Improvisational	Logical	Curious
28	Strategies, Tactics, and Tools	Goals	Mission and Vision

NAVIGATING YOUR PLACE ON THE ADVISER STYLES GRID

In any given client relationship, you may find yourself in different columns across the same attribute at different points in the relationship. You will likely also find yourself operating in different columns or styles within various client relationships. With some clients, you may have the role of team leader, yet you are operating in a sales capacity. With others, you may help a client get to a point of deep clarity through questioning germane to the discernment style, and then take a step to the left and put your advice hat back on to implement.

When reviewing the grid, consider how your clients view you. Not just your best clients, but all of your clients. In which column do you have the most confidence, the most consistent attitude, and the strongest belief in what you do? Regardless of the evolution you wish to make, commit to honing your craft.

Consider having candid conversations with your best clients about what they value most in your relationship. Frame the conversation by explaining that you've been doing some research, and that you are exploring changes that may be taking place in the minds of wealth holders. Ask them to give you feedback about strengths and weaknesses in your business model. Here are some sample questions:

- What has been the most positive aspect of planning you've done, either with my firm or another adviser?
- What has been the most frustrating?
- How would you describe my role in your financial situation?
- Given what you know about me, what do you think I should do more of or less of in my business model?
- What remaining doubts do you have about your wealth or its impact on your family? Where would you turn to resolve the doubts?
- If one thing could change about the complexity that wealth has created in your life, what would it be?

EXERCISE:

Make a photocopy of the Adviser Styles Grid. Starting with attribute number one, work *horizontally across the columns*, one attribute at a time, circling the words that most clearly reflect your attitudes, preferences, and behaviors.

After proceeding through all 28 attributes, choose a different color pen and work across the columns again, one attribute at a time, circling the words that represent attributes you aspire to.

Use the information and sample questions in this book in your data-gathering conversations. Adopt a willingness to get out of your comfort zone and into some deep discovery with clients. Try it a few times and then take some time to reflect and jot down notes about the differences in your clients' experiences, and in the quality of the choices they made.

6 *Why Planning Fails: The Four Key Obstacles and the Confidence Formula Solution*

CHAPTER AT A GLANCE:

Every seasoned adviser has had clients who came close to implementing, but never signed the paperwork. There are countless wealthy families who have engaged smart legal and financial counsel yet are walking around with planning that is incomplete. Many families have completed documents that they don't understand or they've implemented complex strategies but can't articulate the goal the strategy was intended to achieve. The Confidence Formula dissects planning into four strategic layers and helps us get to the root of why planning fails, allowing advisers to diagnose and improve their approach.

A group of high-powered, highly skilled advisers from multiple disciplines come to the table on the client's behalf. The client is smart, wealthy, and has a desire to advance his planning. Conversations take place; numbers are modeled. Flow charts are skillfully drawn and presented.

The wealth holder pays ample fees to best-in-class talent. Yet little or no forward progress is attained. Why does planning for wealthy and high-wealth families so often start off with a bang and slam to a halt, only to be picked up again years later by a different team?

The industry contains countless advisers who possess the integrity, expertise, and people skills to get the job done. So why does every wealthy family we meet lack a complete plan? Why are their experiences so distasteful?

Some say that only advisers who get paid on incentives will keep their eye on the ball long enough for the wealth holder to cross home plate. Some say that a lack of competence runs rampant, and that this is the reason so many families are left with substantial financial, legal, and tax exposure. If it's not being tended to, it must be that the players at the helm don't have the motivation, technical expertise, professionalism, or tenacity to get the job done.

Yet in prospecting, good advisers are frequently stopped cold by a lack of interest from a prospective new client. The wealth holder has already aligned himself with competent people he trusts and therefore considers the work to be done. He doesn't realize he has only achieved two of the four elements required for a successful plan.

In order to make a highly confident decision—one in which the confidence sticks over time—a wealth holder requires four distinct elements: trust, clarity, competence, and management. It is not sufficient for an adviser to excel in one area of guidance and handle the others by

THE CONFIDENCE FORMULA

The Confidence Formula™ = Trust + Clarity + Competence + Management

Our experience indicates that the Confidence Formula is an equation for creating positive planning results. It dissects effective planning into four strategic layers. For scenarios in which planning stalled or stopped, it helps us diagnose the reasons. It also offers a methodology for creating successful scenarios going forward.

default. If the adviser doesn't possess expertise or process in one of the four areas, the missing link must be outsourced to someone who does.

WHY PLANNING FAILS, REASON #1: LACK OF SUFFICIENT TRUST

Trust is the basis for all relationships, and the level of trust a wealth holder is able to afford the advisory team has significant implications for achieving progress in planning. The wealth holder must trust everyone seated at the proverbial table, even those he or she may never personally meet (this could be a technical expert engaged backstage or an institution with whom an adviser is affiliated). Now consider the minds of the affluent. They are approached daily by people who want something from them. They wear skepticism as a protective coat of armor. Trust may be the most difficult thing they have to enlist in planning.

Add to this challenge the rampant abuses of trust in the financial services marketplace. Good, smart people are taken advantage of every day. The mere term "trust" is treated with the casual nature of an object you could purchase at a retail store. Every adviser claims to have it, and most say their ability to establish it is better than the other guy's.

Having an innate ability to build trust is not enough. It is a skill we need to respect, analyze, and hone. The Trust Formula™, as outlined in Chapter 2, offers a way to quantify an adviser's ability to build trust. It gives us a methodology for establishing trust, and for introspectively examining how we, as individuals, can do a better job of facilitating trust in professional relationships.

LACK OF SUFFICIENT TRUST AS AN OBSTACLE IN PLANNING

- The wealth holder must have trust in every participant, not just the key participants.
- Advisers often mistake good relationship chemistry for deeply rooted trust.
- Without a method for measuring trust, how do we know it's there? (See the Trust Formula™ outlined in Chapter 2.)

The most trusted adviser of the future will possess a method for helping the wealth holder tangibly evaluate how trust is being earned and used by every member of the advisory team, as well as an ability to document changes and progress in the trust dynamics present at the planning table.

WHY PLANNING FAILS, REASON #2: LACK OF SUFFICIENT CLARITY

Clarity is defined by the client's utmost confidence in what he or she is trying to achieve. If a wealth holder has clarity around the intent behind a particular planning strategy, it means their vision is so completely apparent it feels as if it is common sense. If you asked them 20 years from now why they acted on a particular strategy or purchased a particular product, they would give you the same answer as right now, today. Also, their answer would represent a vision, not a solution. Raising financially frugal children is a vision. Saving taxes so there's more to fund the family foundation is a solution.

As advisers, it's important to ask ourselves how frequently clients feel that way about a planning strategy we're about to implement. Is their implementation driven by clarity or fatigue? If they don't implement, what caused them to back away from the table?

ADVISER STORY PROVIDED BY SCOTT FITHIAN:

A few decades ago, while I was still getting my arms around why planning fails and how to fix it, I had the following experience. My client had a net worth of $10 million. They owned several hundred acres of raw land and a substantial amount of a particular highly appreciated stock. Based on the fact pattern, I recommended implementing a Charitable Remainder Trust (CRT). After 14 meetings, each considering a different variation of the plan, I was convinced they were ready to move forward. They implemented a few aspects of the plan but they never pulled the trigger on the CRT.

[Continued on Page 53]

[Continued from Page 52]

A few years later, during a planning review, I asked how they felt about their plan. They said, "We're not really sure, we don't understand it." Then I asked how they felt when we originally created the plan and their answer was the same, "We didn't really understand it, we were confused by it all." So I asked another question, "If you were confused, why did you implement some of the recommendations." Their answer, "We were tired and we wanted to stop."

The clients had used implementation as an exit strategy from the planning table. Fortunately, they are still clients and have helped me refine the basis for my methodology over many years. Our conversations are no longer driven by logical fact patterns that only serve to fix tactical issues. They start in a different place, looking at the greater vision for learning how the family wants to leave a mark on the world. As a result, they have implemented a greater quantity of complex strategies than any other client.

Lack of clarity is what draws wealth holders toward or away from the planning table. Before there was any wealth to speak of, they anticipated that money would bring freedom. Instead they are faced with larger and more troublesome questions. Wealth has flooded their lives with an abundance of facts, circumstances, and intertwining decisions.

Their need for clarity is two-fold. First, the wealth holder must have clarity and it must be documented. Second, the documentation must be shared with the full advisory team, and the team must, as a group, possess clarity about the wealth holder's intentions. The document becomes the guidebook for the wealth holder's tactical planning. If the topic, product, or strategy doesn't match the client's documented vision, it never makes it to the planning table.

Lastly, it is crucial to highlight the difference between intellectual acknowledgment of a bright idea and emotional excitement about the bigger goal a strategy achieves. This is the difference between

LACK OF SUFFICIENT CLARITY AS AN OBSTACLE IN PLANNING

- *Advisers must separate a client's intellectual acknowledgment of a great idea from their craving for emotional clarity about the broader intent for their planning.*
- *Tax reduction is an effective sales technique but is not always the wealth holder's key driver. It may get a conversation started, but it often lacks sufficient emotional conviction to get a strategy implemented.*
- *Ask yourself whether tax reduction is the real reason the wealth holder came to you for help. What deeper quandaries are they contemplating?*

intermediate acceptance of a logical set of facts and the true gut-level clarity which drives humans to take action. The primary flaw in planning for emerging-wealthy and high-wealth families is the assumption that sound recommendations made by smart advisers should be implemented. It was a great plan design. Why didn't they implement it? Because they never internalized the root need. They hadn't even clearly identified the problem. Not wanting money to mess up the kids isn't solved by stringent trust language. It's solved by wealth holders' clarity about what they do want the wealth to do for the kids. They didn't implement the obvious plan design because they didn't see it as a solution to their problems. They never bought into it with their hearts and souls, and therefore their wallets and signatures. This is why planning fails.

WHY PLANNING FAILS, REASON #3: LACK OF COMPETENCE

Once trust and clarity are present, the next factor in making a confident decision is competence. Does the current team have the technical expertise to help the wealth holder identify, select, and implement the solution, and manage the result over time? We have all seen decent recommendations poorly implemented to create a catastrophic result. If wealth holders do not perceive—consciously or subconsciously—

LACK OF SUFFICIENT COMPETENCE AS AN OBSTACLE IN PLANNING

- *Every seat at the wealth holder's table must be filled by an adviser with sufficient competence in their particular discipline. With even one weak link, the wealth holder may halt all planning.*
- *Competence is the least frequent reason why planning fails. Many advisers are preoccupied with obtaining additional technical designations instead of tending to their abilities in the realms of clarity and management.*

that adequate competence exists in the seats that are filled, they will eventually retreat from the table without implementing.

Competence, believe it or not, is the least of the wealth holder's worries. It is not the primary reason planning fails. It is not the area in which seasoned advisers require the most self-improvement. In fact, we believe that many advisers have an overzealous preoccupation with improving their technical knowledge. The industry is abundant with tax, legal, insurance, and investment experts. Lack of information or quality information is the least common reason planning fails.

WHY PLANNING FAILS, REASON #4: LACK OF MANAGEMENT

Effective management requires one adviser or firm to take complete ownership for the wealth holder's ability to first achieve clarity and then achieve implementation and ongoing management of the result. Often, there are factions of tenacious, well-intentioned team members but no single adviser in whom the wealth holder has vested explicit authority to manage the team.

We know that an incompetent team will likely produce a poor result, but even worse, a competent team lacking adequate clarity and management will produce a poor result at a high cost.

An effective management process is crucial in all three adviser styles and at both extremes of the wealth spectrum. Effective management includes a systematic method for reevaluating clients' changing needs and mindsets on a regular basis. In the best-case

LACK OF SUFFICIENT MANAGEMENT AS AN OBSTACLE IN PLANNING

- *In the emerging-wealthy and high-wealth markets, the team leader of the future will commit to managing all aspects of the wealth holder's affairs—not just the core disciplines of legal, tax, financial planning, and investment management.*
- *Management will include, for example, overseeing all of the client's money managers, whether or not you manage the assets.*
- *It will also include managing preservation of the family's intangible assets: documenting the wealth holder's value systems and decision-making patterns so they can be shared with future generations.*

scenario, in the affluent market and beyond, there should be an annual fee attached to this review so that it is perceived by the wealth holder as a deliberate exchange of value.

ADVISER STORY:

Charles Hollander, owner of Applied Strategies & Counsel, Inc., in Scottsdale, Arizona, used a true management process to help a client identify and achieve his life dream.

He was a self-made man who had amassed assets of $17 million through the growth of his business. He was referred to me because he wasn't happy with the management of his liquid portfolio of $5 million. At the time, he had investments with three different advisers and he was acting as the point person. I explained to Steve that we would be happy to eventually manage his investments but that we don't make investment recommendations in a vacuum of the bigger picture. I explained our process for strategically managing a person's entire situation in context by first getting clarity about their vision.

Steve was intrigued enough to engage us and we began the discovery process to identify his vision. It turned out that he had always loved the water and had a lifelong dream to buy a large

[Continued on Page 57]

[Continued from Page 56]

yacht and sail around the world. He had never said this out loud. He hadn't even really admitted it to himself. He wasn't sure he could afford it and couldn't begin to figure out how to get away from the business for a long enough period of time.

With his vision firmly in place, we communicated it to the rest of the team. The investment advisers were a bit surprised to find out that beating the market wasn't Steve's primary goal. The CPA was taken aback to learn that extensive tax planning wasn't number one on Steve's radar. It is worth noting that Steve had done a great job engaging best-in-class advisers. They were all extremely technically competent. Yet now there was a common goal to manage toward, and it had all the momentum of being Steve's life dream.

My firm coordinated communication and execution between the logical players—the core CPA and attorney—but we also oversaw the three existing money managers, a business valuation expert, a real estate attorney, and an additional attorney who was a specialist in exit strategies. Once we had built a sound technical plan, we met with Steve's philanthropic advisers to discuss how his vision might affect his charitable commitments. Next we engaged a property and casualty expert to educate Steve and the team about proper insurance coverage from the standpoint of the yacht itself, and liability issues inherent in having guests aboard.

I will never forget how it felt to watch the look on Steve's face as his vision developed into a reality before his eyes. He was nice enough to express the fact that he would have never gotten to this point without a real management process. Someone needed to stimulate and manage his vision while at the same time being willing to look at the myriad pieces required to achieve it. Years later, we were asked to manage all of Steve's investments. That was just the icing on the cake.

COMPREHENSIVE PLANNING: BE CAREFUL WHAT YOU WISH FOR

In high-end planning, we often see self-appointed managers. These are advisers who are skilled at the technical side of creating a plan, commit to managing the pieces to fruition, and who typically have a core competency that becomes a part of the solution at some point—either insurance or investments. The challenge that surfaces is the overused and under-defined term *comprehensive planning*. The term is subjective at best, and unfortunately, so often used in planning that we must assume it is used to describe a variety of intentions and support structures. To the high-end adviser, comprehensive is often defined as ensuring the insurance, investment, legal, business transfer, and tax planning work in harmony. This is a far better result for the wealth holder than they might achieve from juggling a variety of experts themselves. However, the most trusted adviser of the future will define comprehensive management as something altogether different. Comprehensive will include accountability for overseeing every insurance professional of every kind; every money manager, whether or not you manage the assets; all of the CPAs and attorneys; any specialist in play at any given time; the wealth holder's philanthropic advisers; and even his or her bankers.

This management role will account for every facet of the wealth holder's financial life, but it won't stop there. It will address the manner in which their life intersects with their wealth. How will adult children manage and preserve the family's tangible and intangible assets? What mentorship is required? It will include documenting the wealth holder's value systems and decision-making patterns and then sharing them with future generations.

This manager will be appointed by the wealth holder and will therefore have the authority to keep the team in check. With a clear center point of authority, the egos of the brilliant remain at bay. He who allows his ego to flare and stall progress is quickly ejected from his seat at the table, or carefully put back in his proper place by the team leader.

This management concept may cause some to contemplate whether to strive for the most trusted adviser role. Being in this role does not mean you have to take phone calls 24 hours a day or be interrupted on a sailboat in the Bahamas. It does mean you must have a team in place to manage the intricacies, and a high-level person who is accessible when you're not available. In the emerging-wealthy market, you will need a team that goes beyond an administrative or client service person. In the high-wealth market, and as you move up the net worth spectrum, advisers will have to build out a real back office with a variety of technical and support people.

WHY PLANNING FAILS, REASON #5: LACK OF CONFIDENCE

Confidence is created through success in the previous four categories. When all four categories are addressed with skill and elegance, wealth holders achieve forward progress in planning. They make confident decisions that carry enough momentum to make it through even the most challenging and precarious of implementation obstacles.

Think back on some of the choices you've made in life that you made with confidence. They likely still feel like solid choices. Interestingly enough, if a client makes a confident choice that yields a poor result, they're typically willing to live with the consequences. They take ownership for their actions.

DO THE RECOMMENDATIONS FIT THE CLIENT...OR THE ADVISER?

Many advisers believe that if you have the right solution, the client will implement. Whose right solution is it? The judgment about what the adviser deems to be right for the client often carries baggage from previous planning experiences. Advisers have seen similar pain in so many families; they quickly arrive at what looks like the best fix. Not only did they fall short of a full diagnosis, they borrowed a diagnosis from the illness of a different family.

It's like the old saying, "If you have a hammer, the whole world begins to look like a nail." Why is it that most life insurance agents wind up selling insurance as part of their planning recommendations? Why is it that attorneys always find documents that need drafting? Because those solutions fit the advisers' skill sets and comfort zones. And why is it that wealth holders often don't act on what's recommended? Because they want a solution that fits them.

THE MYTH OF CLARITY—LOGIC VS. OWNERSHIP

Why is it that you can present a great idea to the right client and the planning goes nowhere? Their tax exposure is so thick you can almost picture Uncle Sam sticking his fingers into the pie. Their investments are so clearly misallocated you cringe at the opportunities they've already missed. Yet no action ensues. We believe it is because a great answer to the wrong question is useless.

Advisers go into planning thinking the client is looking for a solution. In reality, they're not even sure what the problem is. They're simply overwhelmed with symptoms, a particular point of pain they want exorcised from their lives. What they really need is clarity about what's bugging them, what they want fixed, and why, so they can confidently select a solution. They need help figuring out the shape of the hole before they can even consider what kind of peg will offer a snug fit.

Our profession often confuses logic with acceptance. Rationally, the idea seems like a perfect fit. However, the client needs clarity—their own clarity, not the adviser's. They need to be stimulated to thoroughly think through the problem until they achieve their own ah-ha. This could take an hour, a week, or a year. When the strategy aligns with their point of clarity, from an intellectual and an emotional perspective, smart wealth holders move forward with surprising momentum. Our experience that this type of clarity is best achieved through deep discernment-based discovery.

We believe that in the emerging-wealthy and high-wealth markets, the wealth holder will begin to demand a more participatory discussion in planning. They are not interested in having an adviser summarize the situation, recommend a solution, and press forward toward an outcome. They want the adviser to bring knowledge and wisdom to the conversation. The emerging-wealthy and high-wealth consumers are intelligent and effective decisions makers. They have been thinking about these issues for years, and they want to be part of the solution.

Advisers have a very specific responsibility here. If a wealth holder comes to the table with a definitive request, "I want to give $5 million to each of my kids and the rest to charity," the adviser must be willing to probe deeper and explore the solution.

This is also why the advisers applying the advice style in the emerging-wealthy and high-wealth markets will find their seats placed at the left and right ends of the table, kitty-corner to the wealth holder, not beside him. The wealth holders in the upper two markets are savvy. They're beginning to wonder why advisers think they have all the answers. They don't want to be told what to do. They want to be engaged in a dialogue, and if the dialogue is facilitated by discernment-based questions, there's an excellent chance they'll come to a new conclusion. They might even sign that paperwork you've been saving for years.

Gwen Harvey of BridgeWater in Toronto, Ontario, helped a wealth holder who was stalled in planning gain clarity about her overall intent for her wealth.

> *Mary was a major shareholder at a public company here in Toronto. She had been hired ten years earlier to help the manufacturing company drive shareholder value and had done a tremendous job. Now, with a substantial portion of her shares about to become liquid, she knew that her financial situation would become far more complex. She proactively sought out a great tax accountant and well-regarded tax lawyer and engaged them both. They began to suggest strategies to defer and minimize tax and for asset protection. She was confident the advisers were exceptionally smart and she knew that on paper the ideas were sound ideas but she didn't have conviction about executing them. The strategies under consideration seemed to separate her from the wealth, and the numbers that were identified for the kids and the family foundation were tax wise but philosophically overwhelming. To make matters more confusing, the accountant and the lawyer had different ideas about how to structure things, and Mary had no context for how to choose. When she shared her struggles with a friend in financial services, he suggested she contact me.*

[Continued on Page 62]

[Continued from Page 61]

I shared our process for clarifying vision first, and Mary visibly began to relax. She engaged my firm and we used our wealth intentions process to help her develop an overall plan. I explained that her vision would become a filter through which we could pass specific strategies to assess if each was the right fit.

Using discernment-based discovery, we explored how she wanted to use the wealth. We talked about protecting her financial independence and then worked through her vision for the children and her community. Mary felt confident her needs would be met, yet she was unsure about her adult children's ability to handle large sums. We documented her intent with a written family financial philosophy and included a mentorship structure for the children. We began some of the programs immediately so that if she were to die prematurely, some of their learning would already be underway. Additional phases of mentorship were outlined for the next decade so that ultimately, the children would be ready to receive the substantial sums outlined in the will. We also worked through her philanthropic vision and she decided to reduce the initial allocation for the family foundation. While philanthropy was paramount to her broader intent for the wealth, she wasn't ready to make all of the long-term decisions right then.

Recently, over lunch, Mary reflected on the events of the previous few years. She shared that she felt very at peace with the planning process, including the decisions she made and the legal and tax structures she chose to support them. She felt great about being able to utilize the brilliant ideas offered by the accountant and lawyer she had selected, instead of completely walking away from the table.

MANAGEMENT = PROCESS + METHODOLOGY

Management can be defined as the way in which you systematically deliver the client's ultimate result. Having a process means that you do the same thing the same way every time. Certainly, planning should be sensitive to the unique personality and communication style of the client. However, if we're running a business, most aspects should be rooted in process, and the processes must be documented.

Methodology is the framework that supports process. It provides the step-by-step marching orders for how you implement processes. Done well, it also provides the adviser and the team with the discipline to use the processes that have been created. As entrepreneurs we tell ourselves innovation is the root of our success. This buys us time and allows us to justify life without process. The wealth holder of the future will smell it a mile away.

Many advisers brag to prospective clients about having a planning *process*. There is a grave difference between describing how a client moves through the food chain of planning and actually having a repeatable process. Do you have a list of the questions you ask at every first discovery session? What do you do when you get back to the office after a meeting? And then what? What is the agenda for the second, third, fourth, and fifth meetings? Is it the same every time or does your staff prepare for each meeting from scratch? How do you know if you missed a question or skipped a step? Without documentation, the people we employ to keep us in line have no measurement for whether we even executed the process.

ACHIEVING THE CONFIDENCE FORMULA IN YOUR PRACTICE

Most good advisers execute in each of the four categories at some level. We each exceed or recede in our abilities at particular times with particular clients. This book is about finding that last little bit of potential improvement and stepping toward it. The marketplace is becoming more demanding. The wealth holder of the future will expect more than intuitive ability. This requires taking your greatest strengths and systematically working to improve them.

EXERCISE:

Consider approaching a situation in which the planning has stalled and using this exercise to determine why. Have a conversation with your client about the Confidence Formula: "Jim, we've spent a lot of time reviewing this issue and these solutions. My experience is that every good decision requires confidence. In planning we find that confidence is the sum of a quality experience in four realms: trust, clarity, competence, and management. Let's circle back and diagnose where the gaps are."

Walk the wealth holder through each of the four areas as defined here. Ask probing questions to identify which of the four areas is on shaky ground. When you receive an answer, ask a follow-up question. Delve deeper until you feel you're on ground that has not been covered in previous conversations.

After the meeting, take a few minutes to document the client's thinking and the ah-has they had during the conversation. Why did a particular thought come to the surface during this conversation, when it hadn't previously? What aspects of your behavior caused the wealth holder to reach a deeper level of clarity?

7 *The Most Trusted Adviser vs. the Specialist/Expert*

CHAPTER AT A GLANCE:

Wealth holders have become savvier about who is best suited to manage their transactions and be entrusted with their vantage points. As a result, the patchwork roles that advisers have historically played are being upended. To remain successful in working with people of substantial means, advisers must embrace the distinct difference between the most trusted adviser and the specialist/expert roles, and make an honest choice about where they belong in the wealth holder's planning life.

Picture the proverbial conference room table. Place a self-made business owner worth $10 million along one side of the table. His accountant takes a seat next to him. His insurance agent and money manager (both highly trusted) pull up chairs across from him. His attorneys, all three of them, are seated at the ends of the table.

Did I mention that his CPA has begun to offer financial

products and receive insurance commissions? Also, the money manager recently took the patriarch to lunch to explain that he offers comprehensive financial planning and would like to entertain bringing these services to the table. Over golf last week, the attorney raised concerns about the investment guys who currently have their fingers in the pie. He has a buddy who should probably take a look at the situation.

The table at which the wealth holder hoped to finally gain peace and clarity has begun to look like a dysfunctional family's Thanksgiving dinner. Everyone has their own agenda and no one's quite sure whose agenda is on the table at any given time.

To protect the wealth holder from all of this confusion, a *de facto* gatekeeper steps in—a trusted ally who stands between the client and the financial riffraff. However this protector, often the client's longstanding attorney or CPA, has multiple roles and agendas: to protect the interests of the wealth holder, an ethical obligation to evaluate every potential decision through the eyes of his or her specific discipline, and to defend his or her own turf. As such, many planning decisions remain in a game of ping pong across the advisory table until the wealth holder calls "game over."

KEY CHARACTERISTICS OF A MOST TRUSTED ADVISER

- *Feels so at home in the discernment style of communication that he or she craves a role that demands this behavior*
- *Embraces a leadership role beyond the ego capital of the position and into the challenges of managing team dynamics*
- *Has an internal drive to achieve the Confidence Formula on behalf of the wealth holder*

DE FACTO GATEKEEPER MEETS MOST TRUSTED ADVISER

The most trusted adviser represents an evolution away from *de facto* gatekeeper and toward a defined role with a clear job description. A specific adviser will be chosen on purpose by the wealth holder to be the most trusted adviser. The most trusted adviser's management role will extend far beyond what most advisers currently do or claim to do. In short, the most trusted adviser will have explicit responsibility for implementing all elements of the Confidence Formula (see Chapter 6: Why Planning Fails: The Four Key Obstacles and the Confidence Formula Solution). Also, as wealth holders crave greater fulfillment from their planning choices, they will search for a most trusted adviser who truly has one agenda: wealth holder clarity. Their search will end when they find a most trusted adviser who is at home in the discernment style of communication.

Indeed, the wealth holder is creating division in his own support team, and advisers will find themselves at a crossroads. Step to the right and more fully embrace the responsibilities and activities of a most trusted adviser, or step to the left and delve deeper into a specialist/expert role, perfecting deep expertise in a core discipline.

THE TAIL WILL NO LONGER WAG THE DOG

The natural evolution toward the most trusted adviser role has the power to completely flip our industry's longstanding dynamic of product and service versus client. Historically, wealth holders working through a financial adviser could only get so close to what they were about to buy. The wealth holder was expected to provide data and come back several weeks later to hear recommendations. The in-between part— the formation of both the problem and the solutions—was handled behind the scenes by the professional advisers. Wealth holders could choose action or no action, but they didn't have a structure for influencing how the dynamic played out.

With the evolution and refinement of the most trusted adviser role, wealth holders have regained their rightful power. In this new paradigm, their most trusted adviser comes to the table with facts and specialists, but not recommendations. The most trusted adviser stimulates deep thinking, asking follow-up question after relevant follow-up question. The wealth holder controls, but does not manage, the players. Wisdom surfaces, allowing the wealth holder to gain deep clarity about the use of his or her wealth. Unique to the discernment style of communication—the wisdom is the wealth holder's, not the adviser's.

ADVISER STORY:

Denny Gustin-Piazza, founder and principal of WealthPlanners and Creative Benefit Strategies in Des Plaines, Illinois, helped a wealth holder articulate his vision and hold steadfast to this vision as he navigated various planning solutions.

The client was in his early fifties with a net worth of $14 million. He had three teenage children and had made a commitment to support each of them through private high school, college, and graduate school. At the same time, he had just taken an entrepreneurial move to start his own consulting firm, and had taken a substantial income hit as a result. This was further complicated by a deep passion for philanthropy and a desire to continue his current gifting activity and even increase it over time. Meanwhile, he wasn't getting any younger and needed to keep investing for retirement. When he came to us for planning help, he was very stressed and very troubled. He felt disorganized and worried that any day, one of the balls might drop catastrophically.

We went through a discernment-based discovery process to unload his stressors and convert them to a clearly articulated vision for his wealth and his future. He finally was able to put on paper that he had three very dominant goals, each with a specific price tag. The documentation also allowed him to prioritize his vision.

Together, we met with various specialists to consider solutions. One very well-respected attorney kept recommending a charitable remainder trust because of its favored tax treatment. Instead of getting caught up in the complexities of understanding the strategy, the client was able to consult his documented vision and easily ascertain that tax savings wasn't his primary driver. Eventually he chose a strategy that included a substantial current gift to charity along with the addition of a fixed-income element within his portfolio. The strategy wasn't the fanciest, but it was the best fit. Because he engaged us specifically in the capacity of a most trusted adviser, we were able to evaluate facts and circumstances together. We did not make any recommendations; we

[Continued on Page 69]

[Continued from Page 68]

simply allowed the solutions to naturally emerge. The client felt great during discovery and after making his final decisions. He said that part of his confidence came from the fact that we charged an isolated flat fee for our most trusted adviser services. He felt it demonstrated our commitment to helping him obtain clarity first. The client later engaged us to manage the assets and pays us a typical asset management fee for the work.

THE EVOLUTION OF THE MOST TRUSTED ADVISER ROLE

Historically, few wealthy families have been exposed to discernment-based communication as a behavior pattern in planning. As more families become aware of the discernment style, they will begin to intentionally reevaluate what they want in a most trusted adviser.

For advisers who gravitate toward the discernment style, the most logical seat at the table is the most trusted adviser. The most trusted adviser role will remain most prevalent in the emerging-wealthy and high-wealth markets, because in these realms wealth holders will pay a fee just for the discovery phase of the relationship. It is also where necessity stimulates the demand: people with more money facing more choices and greater consequences to each choice. The most trusted adviser uses the discernment style to help them achieve peace in their decision making.

It's important to note that you can operate in the discernment style without choosing to be a most trusted adviser. However, over the next decade, our experience suggests that advisers will face significant obstacles in trying to engage new most trusted adviser relationships

“It's important to note that you can operate in the discernment style without choosing to be a most trusted adviser. However, you can't be a most trusted adviser without a commitment to using the discernment style.”

without demonstrating interest, commitment, and skill sets for using the discernment style.

For now, most trusted advisers won't have to give up their core disciplines such as an investment practice, insurance business, law practice, or CPA firm. Unfortunately, the economics don't yet exist for successful advisers to be compensated only as a most trusted adviser. For the most part, wealth holders won't pay the substantial fees necessary to make it work.

This opportunity to represent both camps may seem like a

ADVISER STORY:

Chris Jacob, owner of advisory firm Cadeau, in St. Louis, helped a couple who came in asking for solutions to take a step back and first achieve a true vision for their wealth.

Bob attended an estate planning seminar I delivered. He was in his early sixties and worth $16 million. After the seminar he came up and signed up for a free consultation. On the day of our first appointment, he happened to meet with his CPA just prior to coming to my office. When we sat down in the conference room, Bob explained that his CPA felt he needed $4 million of second-to-die life insurance for an annual premium of $40,000 year. Bob wanted to know my thoughts.

I explained to him that I had no idea if he needed insurance or if so, what kind or how much. We talked about the process my firm uses to help people first achieve clarity about their broader vision. Bob agreed to pay a $5,000 planning fee and we began the discovery process. He and his wife, Ann, completed questionnaires about their attitudes and preferences surrounding wealth. We conducted a biographical interview and developed a written family financial philosophy. Halfway through the discovery process, Ann asked, "When are you going to try to sell us something?"

Bob and Ann came out of the discovery process with a completely different view of their wealth. They felt it extended far

[Continued on Page 71]

[Continued from Page 70]

beyond their material assets and into the elements of their character and decision-making patterns that were documented in their written family financial philosophy. They saw the family financial philosophy as a clear statement of intent that could guide their sons to respect and appropriately utilize the family wealth. When their vision was at a clear resting point, we began to shop for solutions. As it turned out, they purchased two substantial policies over the course of our ten-year relationship, with a total premium far beyond what they asked for at the first visit to my office.

Since then, Bob passed away and Ann is still a great client. Sometimes over coffee she talks about those first meetings we had and our initial discovery process. She reminisces about how different it felt to have a planning conversation where the only thing on the table was trust.

contradiction to the bifurcation of the marketplace. The central point is the concept of trust. When the relationship between the adviser and the wealth holder rises above any point of hesitancy or doubt, the adviser can provide solutions and receive commissions without being perceived as lacking objectivity. This is supported by the Trust Formula cited in Chapter 2. When the wealth holder sees your consistent lack of self-orientation, trust increases dramatically.

> “Many advisers have earned the primary position of trust with their clients; yet it’s relished as an achievement rather than embraced as a daily set of responsibilities and tasks. How have they leveraged the trust to help the client push forward in his or her thinking, to achieve his or her ideal plan?”

LIFE AS A MOST TRUSTED ADVISER

Many advisers have earned the primary position of trust with their clients; yet it’s relished as an achievement rather than embraced as a daily set of responsibilities and tasks. How have they leveraged the trust to help the client push forward in his or her thinking, to achieve his or her ideal plan?

The most trusted adviser has the desire and the skill set to move the wealth holder forward with courage. This is not the tenacious herding and leadership on which many advisers have long prided themselves. The most trusted adviser guides the wealth holder to take emotional risks in order to achieve greater depth in their thinking.

Consider the path the wealth holder has been on before they get to the planning table. When self-made people begin to achieve affluence, everything changes in their friendship dynamics. They find themselves with little safe haven to let their guard down about life, wealth, and family; about personal progress or demons. Their friends can't afford to do the things they do and they can't empathize with the wealth holder's family or business issues. "How can I tell Johnny I'm not going to buy him a new BMW when I have five cars in the driveway?" No one's absorbing their thinking or pushing their thresholds.

The wealth holder has trusted their gatekeeper with their financial stories. They sometimes trust their pastor or another confidante with their sacred stories. The most trusted adviser of the future will synchronize these two roles. They will embrace their seat at the table with a lack of bias or self-orientation. They will possess a clear compensation structure and affiliation model that is bulletproof in its support of their integrity. They will take complete managerial responsibility for the wealth holder's total planning life and fiduciary responsibility for any core disciplines they bring to the table.

The most trusted adviser will spend substantial time with the client far before even a whisper of strategy selection or implementation is on the table. This is not planning time, it is bonding time, discovery time. The most trusted adviser will have the skill and the courage to intertwine the wealth holder's tangible financial assets with their journey to clarify and protect their intangible assets, such as character and life purpose. The notion, "Clients just trust me. I don't know how I do it," will no longer be a sufficient communication model. The most trusted adviser must possess a systematic, documented method for helping clients turn complex, painful, and fuzzy issues into clear, confident solutions.

SPECIALIST/EXPERT: A VALUED AND LUCRATIVE ROLE

Many advisers feel at their best in the sales style or the advice style. They derive satisfaction from client intimacy, but it's not the primary reason they enjoy the business. They enjoy the multidisciplinary nature of good planning but have little desire to take managerial responsibility for the total picture, forever.

By nature of its fiduciary responsibility, the most trusted adviser role creates an abundance of opportunity for professionals with expertise in various disciplines. These seats extend into the minute tributaries of products and strategies that today's wealth holder may need to engage for a particular project.

The specialist/expert role is one of great respect, necessity, and prosperity. The wealth holder cannot complete a planning cycle, particularly a complex one, without the aid of one or more specialist/experts. However, if you feel yourself settling into this role as the right role, be aware of the slow shift in your market access.

Wealth holders have gripped the steering wheel of their planning lives for too long. They had never found one soul in whom they could place total trust. As the most trusted adviser role becomes commonplace, the wealth holder will celebrate the opportunity to take a step back from planning. Once the most trusted adviser has helped them to discern their strategic wealth vision, all ideas, facts, and disciplines will pass through the most trusted adviser. The wealth holder will only come back to the table when there's a fork in the road.

> "If you look back over the last five years, how many times have you been referred to the wealth holder's existing CPA, attorney, or CFO for initial buy-in of your potential role on the planning team? For the five years before that, how many times did the handoff occur?"

The most trusted adviser of the future will control all access to the wealth holder. The specialist/expert may still have direct contact with the wealth holder, but they won't have the same quality and texture of interaction they've enjoyed in the past. The most trusted adviser will be seated at the table at nearly every meeting and their presence will be felt in every decision. Indeed, the specialist/expert's future prospective client is the most trusted adviser, and no longer the wealth holder directly.

Perhaps right now, today, it's difficult to believe that this model will become pervasive in planning for families of wealth. We submit to you that the landscape is changing; that more often going forward, the specialist/expert will be handed off to the most trusted adviser. If you look back over the last five years, how many times have you been referred to the wealth holder's existing CPA, attorney, or CFO for initial buy-in of your potential role on the planning team? For the five years before that, how many times did the handoff occur? Times are changing.

Every good adviser will always have a handful of direct client relationships in which they have developed a bulletproof bond. Choosing the specialist/expert role puts you at a point of disadvantage in creating fresh relationships of this nature going forward.

KEY CHARACTERISTICS OF A SPECIALIST/EXPERT:

- *Has a natural desire to learn and master deeply technical planning structures and products*
- *Prefers the cachet of specific expertise over the responsibility of leading the full planning team*
- *Would rather give up some direct relationship access to the wealth holder than become a manager and gatekeeper of the whole process*

Historically, if you were referred by a buddy, credibility was assumed and the proof was in the relationship skills. Going forward, the most trusted adviser's role is to evaluate your technical competency and test your professional reliability. They will tour the recesses of your brain and the back stage of your office.

The specialist/expert's marketing world will also change dramatically. It is imperative to establish relationships with attorneys, CPAs, or other centers of influence. Gone are the days of personal observation marketing, where you can move into new client opportunities over golf or at charitable events. All new opportunities will pass through the most trusted adviser channel.

CIRCLING THE BEND

The bifurcation into the most trusted adviser and specialist/expert camps will initially be most prevalent in the emerging-wealthy and high-wealth markets. To maintain success and growth in traditional financial services business models, one option is to move downmarket into the $1 to $3 million net worth range, or to intentionally avoid moving upmarket into the $10 to $20 million range of the emerging-wealthy and high-wealth markets.

It is important to note that as you move up the wealth spectrum, beyond $20 million of net worth, the concepts presented here simply magnify. The roles remain fundamentally the same, but the moat between the most trusted adviser and the specialist/expert becomes wider and deeper.

Many advisers will choose to ignore these trends. They will approach each future day as they have each past decade. Some will continue operating in the same manner in the face of a changing world, and expect the same results they've enjoyed in the past. The effectiveness of the historic method of doing business with the wealthy is on the decline. We are already heading into diminishing returns. Change is good, especially when you proactively choose for yourself.

8 The Intentional Team Model: The Core Team, the Virtual Team, and the Role of the Specialist/Expert

CHAPTER AT A GLANCE:

For decades, wealth holders have held on tight to advisers they trust as a means of navigating the complexities of wealth. For lack of a better solution, they assembled accidental teams, inviting miscellaneous players to their planning tables at various points in time. These dysfunctional, de facto *teams often lack leadership, communication, and sometimes the right skill sets. The Intentional Team Model gives the wealth holder a clear solution in which the team is built with scrutiny and intention, and is governed by a defined leadership structure.*

You turn on the television set one Sunday afternoon to watch the game, but you can't seem to find the right channel. When you do, the players are behaving awfully strangely. Some are only wearing half their uniforms and some haven't suited up at all. They don't appear to know each other. Some are acting like coaches and some are running around the field. One is dribbling a soccer ball and another is tossing a football. They don't seem to have consensus about how to score. It appears as if they don't even know they're a team. If it weren't so unsettling, it might be humorous. You sit back in your chair, scratch your head and realize that you're not sure what game you sat down to watch in the first place.

One of the greatest dysfunctions in high-end planning is the confusion surrounding the players and dynamics that comprise an effective planning team. When speaking to a prospective client about the need for planning, we hear time and time again, "No, thanks, I've got it all done." The irony of the statement is that no one is actually defining what *it* is. As advisers, we know that it takes a team of professionals to accomplish some form of *it* for the wealth holder. Does the client know this? Does the team know they're a team? What playbook are they working from? Who's calling the plays and who designed them? The wealth holder, so keenly focused on getting *it* done, surrounds himself with a variety of all-stars without realizing what he really needs is an all-star *team*. Without some commonality of a goal, how do we know when our work, even one phase of *it*, is done? Worse yet, it's not the wealth holder's fault. Advisers hear the locker room chatter; advisers have clarity about who should sit at the wealth holder's planning table. Why isn't anyone speaking up?

Wealth holders who have slowly amassed assets over time arrive at affluence with a *de facto* advisory team in place. Some of their team members have been permanent fixtures for decades; some have come and gone over the years due to need, relationship, or competence. In this unintentional team model, who is measuring the "*done*" point? In the era of affluence, longevity and loyalty will no longer be the qualifiers for team assembly. The most trusted adviser

"When speaking to a prospective client, we hear time and time again, 'No, thanks, I've got it all done.' The irony of the statement is that no one is actually defining what *it* is."

will evaluate the wealth holder's planning needs and assemble a team with intentionality and purpose.

If you look to a successful, well-respected corporation for insight, you won't find the top-floor offices filled with an accidental team of executives, several of whom happen to have gotten a job when they were young and played golf with the big guy. Indeed, the design and management of a sizeable estate emulates a corporation, sharing all of its complexities and requiring specific expertise to run it well. Yet the wealth holder holds on tight to the advisers who have been around for years, even when they don't possess the full breadth of talent required. The very industry that was built to serve wealth holders has caused them to be inadequately served. The Intentional Team Model allows clarity to come back to center. When the team is built with strategy, process, and intentionality, the wealth holder can have confidence in its counsel.

THE INTENTIONAL TEAM MODEL

The Intentional Team concept offers a structured, integrated model for managing wealth holders' planning needs over their lifetimes. It is comprised of the Core Team, which is permanent, and the Virtual Team, which is assembled to address specific, temporary needs. The idea is reminiscent of the virtual corporation concept that came in and out of vogue quite quickly. The thought was that companies with specific expertise would come together for specific purposes to accomplish a clearly defined task. This model did not work in the corporate world because many corporations overcomplicated its implementation, failing to grasp the genius of its inherent simplicity. The concept requires all of the players to keep their egos in check. They must play nicely in the sandbox and be happy to leave the playground when their presence is no longer required.

THE CORE TEAM

Led by the most trusted adviser, the Core Team's permanent roles cover four essential areas of competence: tax management, legal management, investment management, and risk management. Core

Team members must be willing to take comprehensive responsibility for their arena even when it means verbalizing a need they can't personally fill, and recommending the temporary addition of a specialist/expert to the team. They are each compensated according to their individual business models.

It is worth noting that the risk manager is accountable for everything that can possibly be insured (life, livelihood, property), but also protection for everything that could topple the wealth pyramid, for example, partnership structures or asset transfers that help the wealth holder manage liability or risk of litigation.

The Core Team is expected to think globally, past the boundaries of their own individual realms embracing an abundance mentality demonstrated in their creativity and their actions. The days of pushing a product solution forward with tenacity are over. The members must behave as true team players, always hoping the other members will shine and caring only about success achieved by the whole.

WHAT DIFFERENTIATES THE CORE TEAM FROM A *DE FACTO* TEAM?

- *The Core Team is intentionally assembled by the most trusted adviser. Professionals are interviewed and references are checked.*
- *Core Team members must define their roles more broadly than in the past. Insurance professionals are responsible for all risk management. Investment managers are responsible for considering illiquid assets, such as real estate, as well as portfolio assets managed by other firms.*
- *The most trusted adviser has more influence over the selection of the players than the wealth holder. The wealth holder delegates the interview process to the intentionally selected most trusted adviser.*
- *The Core Team has a documented vision to address prior to engaging in any billable hourly brainstorming. Saving taxes is not a vision. Transferring work ethic as a key family value is a vision.*

THE VIRTUAL TEAM

If the Core Team is inherently strategic, the Virtual Team is more tactical, coming together for a specific purpose as needed to address a particular planning gap, and later disbanding when the need has been filled. The Virtual Team is typically made up of the most trusted adviser, one or more members of the Core Team, and one or more specialist/experts. As with the Core Team, members are compensated according to their individual business models.

In the *de facto* team models of the past, all headaches and question marks landed at the wealth holder's feet. Now there is a process in place that allows the most trusted adviser to effectively rally a solution. With process comes confidence. When you explain and deploy this model, wealth holders let up on the reins. The most trusted adviser is given more freedom to select the players and execute. The shackles of past planning are released. If you have always wondered whether planning for the affluent really needs to be so difficult, the answer is no. This model is part of the yes.

WHAT DIFFERENTIATES THE VIRTUAL TEAM FROM A *DE FACTO* TEAM?

- *The Virtual Team consists of the most trusted adviser, relevant members of the Core Team, and relevant specialists/experts chosen to address a particular planning gap.*
- *Specialist/experts will be selected by the most trusted adviser with intentionality and as the result of a proactive search.*
- *Team members are selected after the vision is established, not before: vision first, strategy second.*
- *Wealth holders will no longer entertain hot ideas for the sake of the ideas alone.*

REDEFINING LEADERSHIP AND THE CONCEPT OF CLARITY[2]

For a team to perform most effectively, it must have a clear, written statement of the goal it is chartered to achieve. In the Intentional

Team Model, during each planning cycle, the team's goal is clearly defined in advance of billable field time.

Before the teams are even assembled, the most trusted adviser ensures this documentation is in place. Once the planning gap has been identified and clearly documented, the most trusted adviser puts on a talent scout hat, first looking to the Core Team to solve the problem.

In more complex situations, sometimes it's unclear whether a solution exists, or the required expertise is not represented by an obvious role. In these scenarios, the free agency concept comes into play. The most trusted adviser goes out into the open marketplace researching the vast universe of all potential resources.

Once the team comes together, the most trusted adviser distributes the documented vision and briefs the team. When discussions begin with the wealth holder's mantra in hand, there is a tremendous efficiency to the process of idea sharing and the way billable time is spent. The conversations no longer meander around what the wealth holder could do to solve a problem. Strategies that are outlandish based on the personality, risk tolerance, or value system of the wealth holder never make it to the planning table. This clarity frees up creative space in advisers' thinking. Instead of a team of all-stars fumbling around the field, the wealth holder finally has an all-star team playing at peak performance. This is "Clarity^2": clarity in the mind of the wealth holder and clarity across every member of the team about the wealth holder's defined goal.

Historically, leadership has been disguised as coordination and

ADVISER STORY:

Pat O'Connor, co-owner of Blackwood Wealth Planning in Winnipeg, Manitoba, was able to implement the Intentional Team model for a new client who came to him with an existing team of advisers already in place.

The client was a self-made business owner, age 54, with a net

[Continued on Page 83]

[Continued from Page 82]

worth of $15 million. When I was brought into the situation, there were communication issues because the planning had been mostly pursued with the business owner, Jack Swanson, and his wife, Milly, had largely been left out of the process. Also, Jack was burnt out from years of hearing different good ideas from his various trusted counsel. Their planning was stalled and it didn't seem to have much hope of gaining momentum.

I met with the CPA and the Swansons at the same time, and explained my process in terms of a team leader role. The CPA was cautious at first, because he was accustomed to having sales people take runs at his client. But he listened carefully to my approach and eventually began to warm up to engaging me. He actually liked the idea of bringing someone else in so that he could stop half-heartedly playing a quarterback role that he didn't particularly enjoy.

Jack and Milly engaged me to conduct a full discernment-based discovery process to identify their vision. Milly became very energized by the process and it actually had a great impact on their communication as a couple. The existing advisers were able to clearly see the Swansons' vision in writing, for the first time in the history of their relationships. They began to let their guards down, listening more intently to each other's ideas. The collaboration that surfaced was truly inspiring.

When it came time to make decisions about which strategies to implement, their advisers were all standing behind them on the same platform of ideas. It gave Jack and Milly tremendous confidence. They started to actually have fun with the process. In the end, they executed a series of highly effective transactions that had previously felt confusing and overly complex. They were extremely pleased and relaxed during the entire process.

quarterbacking. The most trusted adviser takes an active day-to-day leadership role, seeing this role as primary and not ancillary. He or she must have the desire and the skill set to lead, build, excite, and manage team dynamics. He or she must check ego at the door and have the ability to put others in check as necessary. The most trusted adviser as team leader is not a role of fame or glamour but a skillful and quiet stimulator of consensus and vision.

MOST TRUSTED ADVISER: THE PLAYER/COACH ROLE

To sustain a viable business model, many most trusted advisers will receive consulting fees for their leadership role and will also receive product commissions for providing solutions. Once you have achieved the trust required to truly fill the most trusted adviser role, the wealth holder understands this duality. They know someone's going to get paid for the solution and they'd just as soon have you be the one to receive the compensation—as long as it's both fair and fully disclosed.

The duality of roles may exist in the legal and tax realms as well. A particular firm may have a partner who serves on the Core Team because she has unique expertise in business exit strategies. She may serve as a Virtual Team member in designing the strategy, and guiding the drafting of documents to support it. Some could say this is a conflict of interest—that the attorney is both providing the idea and being paid for the solution. However, when sufficient trust exists, the dynamic is effective regardless of the discipline.

DEFINING YOUR PLACE ON THE TEAM

As you consider the Intentional Team Model, take the time to consider which role feels most natural to you and most appropriate to your skill set, not just from a technical perspective but from the standpoint of relationship capabilities, patience, and process. How are your core talents best offered? In what role can you do the most good for the wealth holder? In what areas are you simply plugging a gap for the wealth holder or skimming by with an incomplete business structure?

If the most trusted adviser role is your ultimate goal, there are several paths. You can apply directly to the wealth holder to become the most trusted adviser, which will require multiple referrals from a variety of trusted allies. A more likely scenario is to first gain a spot on the Core Team, building sufficient trust over time to potentially migrate to the most trusted adviser role. The third scenario is to serve as a Virtual Team member filling a specialist/expert role during a particular planning cycle, and attempting to merge into the most trusted adviser role over time. A lack of visibility and relationship with the wealth holder makes this path the most difficult.

"The demand for the Intentional Team Model calls the bluff of the one-stop shop."

THE SLOW, PAINFUL DEATH OF THE ONE-STOP SHOP

Many large institutions have experimented with offering wealth holders a single place to come for every aspect of their planning. The demand for the Intentional Team Model calls the bluff of the one-stop shop. In the affluent marketplace, the one-stop shop will cease to be viable for four key reasons. First, wealth holders have best-in-class expectations. They have the business acumen to know that no single organization can maintain this level of talent in every discipline. They recognize that top talent often feels stifled under the weight of bureaucracy and sets out to hang its own shingle.

Second, today's wealth holder encounters the need for very specific solution providers. There are so many intricacies to complex planning; a single organization can't possibly house every facet under one roof in a financially viable business model. Third, some of the wealth holder's planning needs are temporary. It isn't cost-effective, and therefore it isn't likely that a single institution would house all of the expertise to address every facet of future planning—both known and unknown.

Last, every wealth holder has existing relationships. In the smoke-and-mirror media barrage of today's financial services marketplace, it is tough to relinquish the one known commodity in his or her planning—the trust he or she places in longstanding advisers.

EXERCISE:

Conduct an introspective exercise regarding the needs of your largest clients. Take out a blank sheet of paper, write a client's name at the top, and divide the page into three columns. In the left column, list the competencies you currently bring to the wealth holder's planning table. In the center column, list the competencies the wealth holder receives from other advisers. In the right column, list the competencies the wealth holder needs and is not currently receiving, or not receiving adequately in terms of attention or quality. Refer to the list printed here to ensure you've addressed all relevant competencies.

Now review each column. In your column, consider which of the competencies you're currently providing that represent your core capabilities. Are you doing the wealth holder a service or a disservice by handling the work? Do you have the adequate skill set, staff, and management process to shine in this area? If not, how can you use the Virtual Team concept to help the wealth holder get what he or she needs? Use the same thought process to work through the center and left-hand columns. What's missing or inadequately addressed by the current team? How can you come to the table and help the wealth holder achieve greater clarity and results in each competency, either through a frank conversation or the introduction of an alternative or additional team member?

PARTIAL LIST OF WEALTH HOLDERS' POTENTIAL REQUIRED ROLES AND COMPETENCIES:

Personal investment management
Qualified plan management
Tax planning
Financial planning
Retirement planning
Estate planning
Business succession, transfer, or exit planning
Life insurance

Property and casualty coverage
Long-term care insurance
Premium health care coverage
Employee group health benefits
Philanthropic planning
Real estate services (tax consulting, legal documents)
Merger and acquisition consulting
Trustee services
Private banking services
Family meeting or retreat facilitation
Family office services
Family coaching or mentoring

Consider this exercise as a potential conversation with current or prospective clients. Help them to see that you care about the total picture of their wealth—not just your role—and that the quality of the fulfillment of each role is crucial to an effective plan. Help the wealth holder to achieve an intentional and high-quality result instead of a potentially precarious *de facto* result.

9 Seats and Compensation

CHAPTER AT A GLANCE:

As financial planning services have become commonplace, fee-for-service models haven't evolved with parallel maturity. Many advisers who are charging explicit planning fees view this revenue stream as a loss leader. A plan without product is not a successful engagement. Wealth holders are beginning to seek out a more believable value exchange. They are consciously aware that clarity is built on trust, and trust can only be present with a clear exchange of fee for service. Ironically, wealth holders are ready to pay for planning; advisers are often afraid to charge.

The financial planning profession has achieved substantial progress since it teetered out of the product provider nest in 1969. The emergence of planning as a discipline has brought greater clarity to the value exchange between adviser and wealth holder. However, much of the industry stalled a bit when it came to creating a fee-for-service structure to house the planning discipline. Most advisers are not charging explicit fees just for the financial planning scope of work, or their planning fees are loss leaders compared to their total revenue-per-client.

Several scenarios exist. Many advisers still provide planning for free in hopes of getting the insurance sale. Some advisers charge fees to manage assets and include the planning in this single bulk fee. Some charge planning fees, but the fee is not commensurate with the promised scope of work. Often even the wealth holder doubts it's enough to cover a full planning process.

We know in our hearts and our intellects that an explicit exchange of value requires clear communication and a defined price tag, yet many advisers have not yet achieved a business model in which their behavior reflects their subconscious belief system. Much of this may be connected to a lack of confidence or process. If I charge a fee, I have to do the work. If I charge a fee, I must be able to clearly document what I'm charging for. I must be able to articulate a compelling value proposition for my planning process. If I charge larger fees, I might scare the guy away and blow the insurance sale. If I'm going to manage a nice chunk of assets, I don't need to stand on ceremony and charge a separate fee for planning. I think I'll hold off on that for awhile. Things seem to be working just fine the way they are.

We submit to you that there is no other profession besides financial services that provides such detailed work, requiring substantial expertise and integrity, in the hope of being compensated for it later, during a different and very specific facet of the relationship. Picture a wealth holder sitting down with a renowned architect and a luxury homebuilder. The wealth holder tells them to build a top-notch house

“We submit to you that there is no other profession besides financial services that provides such detailed work, requiring substantial expertise and integrity, the hope of being paid later, during an entirely different and very specific facet of the relationship.”

to his liking, using the best talent and materials they can find. At the end of the 18-month process, they'll all come back to the table and he'll decide whether to buy the house. How long does it take the architect and the builder to back away from the negotiating table?

How can we be stewards of a process we're not explicitly and sufficiently paid to execute? What other professional discipline allows the first encounter with a new client to be a loss leader? If the wealth holder isn't paying a fee, what is their expectation for quality? Wealth holders understand value exchange. They engage in dozens of fee-for-service relationships daily with their vendors, domestic help, and medical professionals. What do they expect from professionals who give their greatest talent away for free? And how committed are they to a process that either lacks clear definition or is so good it doesn't cost anything?

DANCING THE DYSFUNCTIONAL DANCE

When wealth holders come into a relationship paying a fee that seems unbelievably small in relation to the work at hand, or paying no fee at all, consider their mindset and commitment level. They're not agreeing to plan, they're agreeing to test you. Why not stick a toe in and see how the water feels? What have they got to lose? On the other side of the table sits a professional who just agreed to do work for less than he or she is worth on the open market. What emotion is the adviser bringing to the table? Fear? Lack of confidence? Consider the dynamic that was just created. The wealth holder has one eye casually on the diagnostics and the adviser is hooked up to an oxygen tank of financial fumes in hopes of a huge payday that is months or years away. Two intelligent successful people have just engaged in a dysfunctional dance that may spin, dip, and twirl for months or years at a time.

THE ACCIDENTAL BARTER SYSTEM

When wealth holders enter any business relationship, they expect a financial exchange to occur. Even without a defined price tag, there's an implied exchange of commerce in play. In the financial services realm, the adviser has agreed to stick around for a while and serve up intellectual capital. The wealth holder has agreed to show up physically and mentally in hopes of furthering planning. The two parties just engaged in an inexplicit, uncommitted barter, a barter for the continuation of the relationship.

Just as the adviser has attempted to remove the financial barriers to entry, he or she has created a relationship roadblock. If you're smart and do good work, wealth holders can't figure out why you're working for free. It makes them uncomfortable. If wealth holders have to question a professional's motivation on any level, the questioning presents a natural obstacle to decision making. As the work increases in intensity, quality, and duration, the question mark becomes larger than life. The pending product sale becomes an elephant in the room. It stands between the wealth holder and the adviser, creating intense suction, eliminating the perception of objectivity like a giant relationship vacuum.

Effective barters are pre-quantified. Exactly what intellectual capital, man-hours, or tangible goods are being exchanged? With clarity comes confidence. When all parties to the relationship know the rules of engagement, they can put those rules aside and focus on the task at hand. When any portion of that communication is inexplicit or unclear, the parties never fully leave the negotiating table to enter the workroom. The question marks are always present, often becoming so distracting they kill the relationship dynamic completely.

It's important to note that many advisers who manage money and charge asset management fees are likewise engaging in this unintentional barter. A common practice is to charge a 1 percent asset management fee and to include the financial planning services in that 1 percent. There is no communication about what portion of the 1 percent is being allocated to the planning services. What happens when the market causes downward pressure on asset management fees? Now the adviser has to charge .75 percent or .5 percent to remain competitive. Can he or she still afford to do the financial plan? Which portion is being squeezed—the quality of the plan or the quality of the investment advice and service? If the plan is so good, why not ask the wealth holder to pay for it? If it's not, why is it being offered at all?

THE POWER OF A CONFIDENT VALUE EXCHANGE

Picture this. A cleaning service shows up at your house unannounced. They mention the names of several of your neighbors whom you know and trust, and ask to clean your house to see if you like it. They're building their business and you're just the type of client who fits their service model. It feels uncomfortable. Shouldn't everyone get paid for their work? They persist. You accept. A week later, they're still cleaning. You've never seen anyone work so hard; yet they won't accept payment. Don't worry, they say, they'll be compensated plenty in the end. You wonder where all that money's going to come from. The next day, you get home from work and they've been grocery shopping and cooking. They took your dog to the groomer and did your laundry. At this point, you have no idea what services they offer and how much it'll cost you. The work looks good but the commerce confusion is overwhelming. You politely cut a check for what seems reasonable and back out of the deal. It was far too vague and far too good to be true.

"Without full compensation disclosure, complete trust is simply not possible, and without trust, deals don't come to fruition."

In contrast, when a professional relationship begins with a clear fee-for-service value exchange, certain things happen. The adviser demonstrates confidence in what he or she is bringing to the planning table. The wealth holder makes a clear and committed choice to be a part of the process. It's far easier to help someone who wants to be helped. By charging an explicit fee just for planning services, one that is commensurate with your expertise and scope of work, you've taken yourself out of the sales model and into the advice model. Now, let's make sure the value exchange plays out.

Now that we have two people who've agreed to do business together, what is the business at hand? At the end of the proposed

ADVISER STORY:

David Parks of Keel Point LLC in Arlington, Virginia, worked with a client to create a mutually beneficial fee structure.

About 18 months into our relationship, we sat down with Jack to discuss the family office and investment management services we had been providing. Our goal was to find out what was working well in his mind, what needed to be changed or improved, and then agree on a fee for the following 12 months. Jack had always been very fee averse, so I was anticipating a struggle. He said he was very pleased with our work and also provided some great feedback in areas that he would like handled differently.

Then the conversation took an interesting turn. He asked us if he was a profitable client for us. At the time, he had a net worth of $120M and was paying us $150K a year for planning with a separate additional fee to manage some of his assets. I shared with him candidly that his situation wasn't all that profitable for us. Due to the complexity of his financial makeup, our work on his behalf was incredibly time intensive and required the focus of many of our top people.

This conversation led to a series of discussions about his desire to become a good client for us by designing a mutually beneficial fee-for-value exchange. We started with a group discussion with his wife, their adult children, and Jack's siblings to discuss their impressions and needs. Then we set up individual meetings between Jack and each of the Keel Point team members that had been working on his behalf. This also gave us an opportunity to help him examine the full breadth of our capabilities, beyond what he had already engaged us to do. He appreciated being invited backstage to learn about our processes, and he clearly communicated where he derived value. He even helped to restructure how we delivered services and reporting to his family, so that the package felt more valuable to him. At the end of the

[Continued on Page 95]

[Continued from Page 94]

process, he suggested an annual fee that was twice what we had started with.

Jack has been an enjoyable and profitable client for many years now. He has also become a great referral source. Our entire team learned from this experience. It reinforced our belief that good clients want to engage in fair business structures; all we have to do is have the courage to ask the questions.

planning cycle, what value will the wealth holder derive? How will you know when you're done? What other advisers or products will come into play during the engagement? What will be the next point of assessment for additional scopes of work? Lay it all on the table. When was the last time you met a self-made person who preferred a relationship interlaced with secrecy and two-way mirrors? Confidence is contagious. Make yours part of your value exchange.

WHAT THE INSURANCE CONTRACT SAYS ABOUT COMPENSATION

Margins are built into the insurance contract to compensate the person who brings the product to market. These dollars are allocated for the selection, placement, and post-sale service of the product. A legal obligation is engaged when the adviser delivers the policy. By executing the contract, the adviser is agreeing to be a party to that contract. The revenue generated from the sale obligates the adviser to service the product for life. Unfortunately for the wealth holder, the insurance contract doesn't define the parameters for appropriate post-sale service.

When planning is provided for free in lieu of a pending insurance sale, future revenue is, in essence, borrowed to pay for current time and talent. Another possibility is that commissions from past sales are consumed to cover current overhead. As such, there's little or no money left to provide the post-sale service that the contract obligates the seller to provide.

In the affluent market and beyond, we believe adequate service includes an annual review of every policy. If this isn't necessary, why are agents constantly finding old policies that no longer serve the intended purpose? The person who sold it didn't service it. He or she didn't stick around to see if their promises would come true for the wealth holder. Is it any wonder why life insurance has a tainted reputation?

It is worth noting that if the most trusted adviser provides the selection, placement, and post-sale service of the insurance product, he or she can receive the commission compensation without jeopardizing the most trusted adviser role. Since the insurance contract is structured to include commission compensation, foregoing this compensation in lieu of a higher fee-only exchange results in redundant expense to the wealth holder—they pay for the same value twice.

COMPENSATION AND LIABILITY

Industry regulators have outlined three standards of liability for financial advisers. At the bottom of the food chain is *negligence*. If you are simply selling products and not offering any planning, this is your litmus test. As long as there is a logical fit between the product you select and the consumer's needs, the law says you've done just fine.

The second level of liability is *suitability*. Suitability requires the adviser to perform some due diligence surrounding the wealth holder's financial position and needs. This standard applies to advisers who offer planning but don't charge planning fees.

The highest standard an adviser can be held to is that of *fiduciary*. This standard carries an explicit legal obligation to do what is right for the client. It obligates the adviser to represent the wealth holder from the wealth holder's perspective. It involves a written contract with a commitment to perform specific services representing the wealth holder's interests. By accepting a financial planning fee, the adviser agrees to compare and contrast ideas and products, not solely examining one solution or one manufacturer. They must evaluate options and bring only the most appropriate solutions to the planning table.

The fiduciary standard is also held to advisers charging fees to manage assets. If advisers are not separating the financial planning fee from the asset management fee, there is a legal grey area about whether their financial planning services are held to the same standard. We believe that once an adviser has behaved in a fiduciary capacity in a relationship, he or she can't ethically back away from this level of accountability.

MAKING THE TRANSITION TO AN EXPLICIT, FEE-FOR-SERVICE BUSINESS MODEL

Soon, competitors will have frank conversations and justifiable reasons about why they are charging planning fees. They will poke holes in your business model to gain competitive advantage. The last one to the table will have to fight the hardest for his or her seat.

One conversation to have with existing clients is about fiduciary accountability. Explain the three standards of liability and ask which level they'd like their team to be accountable to. Explain why you have chosen to be held to a fiduciary standard on their behalf. In essence, they are paying for the right of representation in the financial planning process.

Note that these conversations can help advisers transition from a no-fee to fee basis. They can also help to transition from very minor fees to a fee structure that is more commensurate with the time and expertise you're allocating to planning services.

Take these conversations one step further by outlining the services you currently offer and the revenue streams that result. Gain a comfort level in being candid with your clients regarding compensation. Industries change. Wealth holders know this. Planning used to be simple. The era of affluence has brought greater complexity to the quantity and type of decisions that planning requires. Wealth holders appreciate the agility with which their trusted counsel can acclimate. They're willing to be part of the process as long as the story is sound. Help them become better-educated consumers. Help them to decipher the stories they're hearing from other professionals, even their buddies.

Take pride in the fact that you are acting on the cusp of a changing industry; that you see the turmoil ahead and you're creating a business model that will survive with integrity, profitability, and relationships intact. Explain the downward pressure on commission income and the necessity to clearly separate planning from product. Find me a successful individual or business owner who can't see the merit in this conversation.

As the financial services industry evolves, and product compensation on the insurance and asset management side is further squeezed, advisers with the greatest ability to articulate and demonstrate their value proposition will prevail. A primary factor is having a logical, fair compensation structure that facilitates trust in your relationships and can withstand scrutiny from any angle.

THE ADVISER STYLES AND COMPENSATION

At the planning table of the future, the manner in which an adviser requests compensation will directly correlate to the seats he or she is invited to fill. Generally speaking, the sales model is considered to be a product-focused role compensated via commission revenue built into the manufacturing of the product. These advisers will be invited to sit across the table from the wealth holder.

Compensation for advisers operating in the advice model comes from explicit planning fees or product commissions. These advisers will be invited to sit kitty-corner from, not beside the wealth holder. Increasingly, advisers will be questioned if their planning or consulting fees are too low to be commensurate with their work product. Their fee levels will inadvertently decrease their professional stature, causing others at the table to perceive them in the sales model.

The discernment model is a relationship-focused model. Typically, this adviser is compensated by more substantial consulting fees and, most likely, by product commissions or asset management fees (as mentioned elsewhere, this is because the marketplace is not ready to pay sufficient fees for advisers to survive on planning fees alone). This adviser is the most trusted adviser, and as such takes a seat directly to the right or left of the wealth holder on the same side of the table.

10 *What Now?*
by Todd Fithian

This book concludes with a logical question. What now? If you see what we see, what can you do to take action in your practice and in the planning lives of your clients? The first point of progress is to acknowledge that the landscape is changing, that the seats at the wealth holder's planning table are indeed being redefined. The consumers of our products and services are defining our roles for us.

As you continue to absorb the material presented here, we ask you to consider a simple opportunity. Until this point, our industry has guided its own evolution. Now more than ever before in history, we as advisers have the power and the tools to create change. We can be more intentional stewards of wealth holders' planning experiences. We can be more intentional about how our business plans, firm structures, and service offerings affect the trajectory of wealth in this country.

This book offers perspective on the available roles so that you can begin to explore your best fit. It allows you to diagram the future of your practice, being clear and candid about what you do and don't do for a living. It allows you to structure a total service model in which you bring the missing players to the table. Imagine an abundance mentality in which a specialist/expert operating in the sales style introduces a most trusted adviser to his or her best client of 20 years. This is just one example of the mark we can leave on our industry.

Everything presented here speaks to a whole new landscape of opportunity for everyone in our profession. If you feel at home in the sales style, acknowledge that the roles on the wealth holder's team are changing. Clearly identify and communicate the role you wish to play. There will always be a need for the sales role at the wealth holder's planning table. As you move upmarket, consider that your client will become the wealth holder's other advisers, and no longer the wealth holder directly.

If you choose to operate in the advice style, consider how you want to position and build your business. Take a step back and design a structure for managing the wealth holder's total situation and complete team—no longer the vague *comprehensive planning* model of the past. Decide whether the most trusted adviser role is the right role for you. Learn how to become a more thorough steward of a family's broader intent for their wealth. Build out your virtual team members and ensure the wealth holder is cared for at every angle.

For some, we hope that reading about the discernment style has left you feeling like you fell asleep and woke up at home. Rest assured that wealth holders in the emerging-wealthy and high-wealth markets are looking for this style and for the most trusted adviser structure. Up until now, this role was vaguely available to the wealth holder through their attorney, CPA firm, or family office structure. The concepts presented in this book allow it to be pulled into the entrepreneurial realm, thereby broadening its awareness and reach. These are exciting times.

WEALTH AS A MAGNIFIER

In our one-on-one work with families in the high-wealth market, we are seeing their heightened sensitivity to do what's right in planning. Should they buy a third home or donate that extra $3 million to charity? People are paying attention to wealth holders' choices, placing their decisions under a magnifying glass of public opinion. As advisers, we must have compassion that wealth brings complexity to the lives of the people we serve. We have an obligation, and now a methodology, for helping them to discern their own best choices. If we use deep discovery to create clarity in the privacy of their own thinking, they can move forward with confidence about their choices.

WHAT NOW?

For those of you who want to implement some of these concepts and structures in your practice, start by considering who you want to be and what your business should look like. Take time out of the office to sit down and sketch it all out. Then identify your ten best relationships and have candid conversations with them. Use the exercises and questions provided in the preceding chapters. Remember that wealth holders want to be part of this process. They trust you and hope you'll evolve with them. Share some excerpts or concepts from this book. Allow the conversations to flow freely. Simply initiating the discussions demonstrates that you are thinking ahead on their behalf, that you're interested in creating more satisfying planning experiences.

A GIFT FROM SCOTT

"*What now?*" was also the shot heard 'round the world for hundreds of people when Scott was diagnosed with pancreatic cancer on June 21, 2005. I had already taken the post of CEO at the Legacy Companies at the time, yet neither of us ever imagined it without him. My brother Scott was one of the greatest visionaries the financial services industry has ever seen or experienced. This is not just a proud brother speaking. Like all things true these days, all you have to do is Google his name to witness what I saw during thousands of presentations to professional advisers, charitable organizations, and wealth holders over two decades.

Scott spent the last year of his life completing this book, intent on documenting his vision so that advisers and wealth holders could carry it forward with authenticity and honor. Many described Scott as having a sixth sense—an ability not only to see trends, but to feel them. He was a student of people, interaction, and relationship. When Scott and I teamed up in 1995, he called me into his office to share his vision. He said that the adviser/consumer relationship needed to change. In his own practice, he saw that the traditional model of providing solutions and strategies didn't relieve the wealth holder of their greatest burdens. We began to develop a methodology that did.

Back then, when Scott gave keynote presentations at major conferences, people looked at him in awe—it sounded so right yet so out of reach. They couldn't see as far forward as he could, yet for Scott, it was already happening. Fast forward to today, where it is not uncommon to see a psychologist speaking at a financial planning conference or to find an article on trust building in an industry trade magazine. The increased awareness brings greater acceptance of the discernment style and therefore offers an opportunity for advisers and for wealth holders.

The process of getting this book published has allowed me to step back and observe. It's one thing to believe wholeheartedly in what you're doing and quite another to see tangible evidence that thousands of others believe it too. We decided to add this chapter so that those of you just getting started on this work could feel confident: Scott's passing is not the end of an era, it's the beginning of an opportunity.

So once again, this book concludes with a logical question. What does the future of your business look like? What is the nature and structure of the relationship between you and the wealth holder? Over the last 15 years, we have personally helped thousands of advisers address and answer these questions. Wealth holders are not only in need of these changing behaviors, they are asking for help. However you choose to address it, do so with conviction. Which is the right side of the table for you?

Reflections from Scott C. Fithian April 2, 2006

WHAT IS LEGACY?

Sometimes life affords us the luxury of becoming a slow-motion observer of the physical world occurring before our eyes. I used to sit on my back porch all the time without noticing the hummingbirds. Now I know how many of them make their daily journey to our feeder, what time of day they get hungry, and the direction from which they approach their afternoon snack. I realize the joy of sitting completely still—a state in which my existence in relation to nature is irrelevant.

How would you express yourself to people if you suddenly faced the possibility of your own mortality? The clarity of thought that presents itself in that realm is, in and of itself, a blessing. Consider the lives you've touched, and the lives those people have touched as a result.

We work in an industry that tosses the word legacy around like a beach ball. What is legacy? What is this intangible that we claim to help our clients preserve?

Who will Grandpa Charlie be to the great-great-grandkids: the guy with all the money, or the soul who embraced charity even when his own luck was down?

The term legacy has been overmarketed. Its very meaning has been stolen. As financial advisers, we help people make life-changing choices. If they make the wrong choice, it can ruin their lives. It can ruin their children's lives. The mere fact that the choices are about money has given the measurement of a successful legacy a monetary connotation.

We've all stood around in a group of advisers where someone is bragging about the size of the case they just closed. What's the legacy of that transaction? What is the legacy of the work that was done? Where does the responsibility end? Is pride in our work about saving taxes or enhancing the lives of the families we serve? Which column gets a checkmark when we stimulate a sudden influx of cash into an untrained heir's hands?

Everyone has a deterrent to living life fully in the present—an attitude, a relationship, a partnership. Some have the luxury of having theirs diagnosed; others meander for decades without seeing theirs. There are so many things we do every day that are simply life's noise. We respond to others' noise and create new noise. We do it subconsciously and on purpose, building a buffer between our actions and the real stuff life is made of. Everyone does it, but our obligation to stop doing it is much greater.

The gift we owe our clients is a wake-up call to live in the present—to create their legacies now with intentionality. The first step is to splash a little cold water on the core of our own thinking. How well are we serving? What is the story we're telling? Is it true? Is it the best we can do?

The planning you facilitate today will affect hundreds, if not thousands, of descendants of each wealth holder's family. The wealth you've preserved will land in someone's hands. It will drive their days and possibly invade their nights. The legal documents and the life insurance policies aren't enough. As much as the industry has convinced itself, this is not legacy. So what is?

LEGACY IS DOING THE RIGHT THING, NOT THE EASIER ONE

Patriarchs say they don't have time to plan. Advisers need to have the intestinal fortitude to take a stand. Nothing is more important in life than caring for the tangible and intangible assets of their families.

Procrastination is the cancer of our modern-day society. Everything can wait until tomorrow. Together we can cure the lack of urgency in planning. Don't let them wait. Become passionate about getting clients to the planning table to execute their decisions. There is nothing more limiting in one's daily thinking than a lack of resolution about money and family. Wealth holders wear it as a private ball and chain. Help them release these burdens. Have the courage to lead them to action. That is legacy.

LEGACY IS HELPING WEALTH HOLDERS FIND THEIR ULTIMATE ENDS

The best decisions in life are made in view of one's ultimate end. Yet our society rewards decisions made based on intermediate ends. It's better to get it done fast than fully. We must redouble our conviction in helping clients get to their ultimate ends in decision making, to dig deeper into the why behind their planning. The why isn't investment returns and tax bills. The why is about people and character and impact.

There is something in the human body that wants to know that having been here has made a difference; it's part of our physical makeup. Advisers say clients don't want to get into the soft stuff. I say they don't know how. We wield tremendous power in our clients' lives. The power of relationship. What kind of steward are you of that power? Beyond making sure the money's well managed and the tax bill is gone, what else is there?

Clients subconsciously sense their life purpose, but they can't quite grasp it. People need to connect with the stories and experiences of their past in order to gain clarity about their present. Wealth holders need someone they can trust and confide in to have those conversations with. They need a nonjudgmental environment in which they can rethink and elaborate on their life experiences without fear of reprisal. An opportunity for stillness paves a pathway for conscious action. Bring the tools for deeper thinking to their doorsteps. Make the journey together. That is legacy.

MORE THAN LISTENING, LEGACY IS HEARING

If every adviser was as good at listening as he or she claims to be, the world would be a whole lot quieter. We all pat ourselves on the back for being good listeners. If we brag about our strengths, we'll never seek to enhance them.

Commit to asking more and better questions. Pause and absorb the answers. Embrace a beginner's mind. Hear without listening for a solution. Let time stand still. Take in the tone of their voice, the careful selection of their words, and the stories in their eyes. Listen with all your being and all of your senses. How can you be a better steward of the intimacy clients are sharing? Listen timelessly. That is legacy.

LEGACY IS ABOUT THE HERE AND NOW

It is about behavior, about how you live in this world rather than how you leave it. To be intentional about your legacy, you must know your purpose.

Human nature is to defy our own mortality. Yet in doing so, we deny our legacies. We are creating our legacies every second of every day. With or without intent, it's being formed—reputation, relationship, experiences, stories. Every word we speak and every decision we make. Each day we skirt around this reality is another day lost in the opportunity to shape it with intent.

So much of our work focuses on the future. It justifies our dissociation from the here and now. The dysfunctionality is mutual. Our focus on the future allows our clients to keep off their own present. Instead of waiting your whole life to get to a point where you can look back and be proud of what you've achieved, why not stop in your tracks and look forward? Be the father, the mother, the business owner, the parent you want to be. Change your trajectory. Who are you? Who do you allow clients to be in your presence?

Help clients stop their worlds from spinning and peer into their greater purpose for existence. What are the values they're passing on to their children? What stories should be documented? What is the texture of their family culture?

Legacy is heritage and heritage is tradition. Traditions are actions captured. Legacy is the most important tool any human possesses. The world will go on forever after we're gone. How will each of us positively impact its trajectory? That is legacy.

People fear change. As advisers, we convince ourselves that our businesses will survive all this. Our relationships will supersede the tidal wave of discontent in the mind of the wealth holders. This stuff is really important—for everyone else.

Let fear bubble to the surface. Make it your mirror. As entrepreneurs, we've all faced hard times in which our backs were up against the wall. Doing nothing wasn't an alternative, so we figured out some way to get through the obstacle. We owe it to our clients to do the same, to discontinue the prominence of our society's preoccupation with money, on future absent presence.

Society's major disconnect is the attachment of wealth to life. We see them as far too interconnected. As advisers, we must restore a focus on life first, wealth second. Wealth is a topic, not a tradition. In the final hours, human connection is all that matters. That is legacy.

Index

Advice style, 14–15, 17, 24–26, 28–32, 34–36, 40, 42, 45, 61, 73, 100
Attribute, 45–48
Barter, 91–92
Behavior, 15, 31, 40–41, 45, 64, 66, 69, 90, 106
Chair, 8, 12, 23, 44, 65, 78
Clarity, 21–22, 28–29, 36, 43–44, 47, 50, 52–55, 58, 60–61, 64, 66–67, 69–70, 78–79, 82, 86, 89, 92, 101, 103, 105
Clarity^2, 81–82
Commission, 17, 30, 33, 66, 71, 84, 95, 96, 98
Communication, 3, 11, 13, 16, 19, 24, 29, 32, 35–36, 59, 63, 66–67, 69, 72, 77, 83, 90, 92
Compensation, 4, 6, 8, 13–14, 17, 25–26, 30, 33, 45–46, 72, 84, 91, 93, 95–98
Competence, 50, 54–55, 59, 64, 78–79
Confidence, 8, 17, 39, 41, 45, 47, 50, 52, 54, 57–58, 61–62, 64, 66–67, 69, 73, 79, 81, 83, 90–93, 95, 101
Confidence Formula, 49–50, 64, 66–67
Confusion, 7, 29, 43, 45, 53, 66, 78, 93
Core Team, 79–82, 84–85
CPA, 12, 33, 59, 65–66, 70, 73–74, 83, 100
Credibility, 15–17, 46, 74

De facto, 66, 77–78, 80–81, 87
Discernment-based, 3, 19, 27–29, 36–37, 40–41, 60, 62–63, 68–69, 83
Discernment style, 14, 21, 24–28, 30–32, 35–39, 42, 45, 47, 66–67, 69–70, 100, 102
Discovery, 2–3, 17, 20, 41, 48, 58, 60, 62–63, 68–72, 83, 101
Emerging-wealthy market, 13, 26–27, 34–37, 39, 56–57, 60–61, 63, 75
Fee, 14–15, 17, 24–26, 30, 33–34, 46, 50, 56, 69–70, 84, 89–98
Fiduciary, 7, 30, 72–73, 96–97
Fithian, Scott, vii, 28, 52, 103
Fithian, Todd, viii, 99
Gatekeeper, 66, 72, 74
High-wealth market, 3, 13, 27, 34–37, 39, 50, 54, 56–57, 60–61, 63, 69, 75, 100–101
Ideas, 3, 14, 17–18, 22, 35, 38, 61–62, 73, 81, 83, 96
Incentive, 4–6, 25, 33, 41, 50
Independence, 2, 4–6, 24, 34, 62
Intent, 1–3, 6, 9, 12, 19–20, 27, 29, 42, 45, 52, 54, 61–62, 71, 77, 79, 81, 100, 102, 104, 106
Intentional Team, 77–79, 82, 84–85
Intimacy, 6, 16–17, 22, 29, 35, 38–39, 46, 73, 106
Lawyer, 15, 23, 61–62
Legacy, 7, 21, 103–107
Liability, 13, 25–26, 30, 59, 80, 96–97
Management, 46, 50, 55–59, 63–64, 66, 69, 79–80, 86, 92, 94, 97–98
Marketplace, 3–4, 6–7, 13, 26, 29, 31, 33–35, 40, 51, 64, 71, 82, 85, 98
Methodology, 36, 50–51, 53, 63, 101–102
Model, 2–4, 7–8, 11, 14–15, 24–25, 29, 31–33, 43–47, 72, 74–75, 77–81, 84–85, 89–90, 93, 97–98, 100, 102
Momentum, 32, 44, 57, 59–60, 83
Most Trusted Adviser, 4, 12, 14–15, 20, 29, 34–35, 37, 52, 56–57, 65–75, 78–82, 84, 96, 98, 100
Negligence, 96
Obstacle, 27, 29, 43, 51, 54–57, 67, 69, 92, 107
Organization, 85, 102

Planning Horizon, 18–21
Process, 4, 13, 21, 24, 32–33, 37–38, 41, 46, 51, 55, 58–59, 62–63, 68, 70–71, 74, 79–84, 86, 90–91, 93, 95, 97, 101–102
Quarterback, 83–84
Questions, 3, 5, 7, 16, 19, 25, 27–29, 32, 35–38, 41, 44, 47–48, 53, 63–64, 95, 101–102, 106
Relationship, 2, 6, 8–9, 13–17, 22, 26, 28, 31, 33–35, 40, 45–47, 51, 69, 71, 74, 78, 84–85, 90–95, 97–98, 102, 104–106
Reliability, 15–17, 46, 75
Sales style, 14, 17, 24–26, 29–33, 36, 40–41, 45, 73, 100
Salespeople, 6, 7, 22, 24, 29, 32–34, 42, 44
Seat, 5, 7, 11–14, 22, 25, 34–35, 44, 55, 57, 65, 69, 72, 97–98
Specialist/Expert, 12, 14, 17, 65, 73–75, 80–81, 85, 100
Suitability, 32, 96
Table, 1–8, 11–26, 28, 30, 32–36, 38, 40, 42, 44, 46, 48–58, 60–74, 78, 80, 82, 84, 86, 90–100, 102, 104–106
Training, 27, 44, 46
Trust, 15–17, 19, 33, 35, 50–52, 54, 64, 68, 71–73, 77, 84–86, 89, 93, 98, 101–102, 105
Trust Formula, 15–17, 22, 51, 71
Virtual Team, 12, 79–81, 84–86, 100